GIVEN IN MEMORY
OF
ROBERT F. PECOR

GREAT
BATTLES
THROUGH
THE AGES

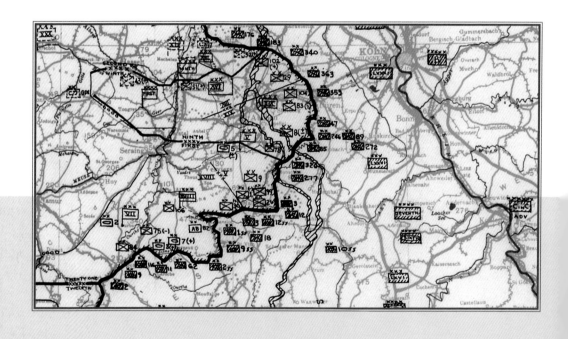

BATTLE OF
THE BULGE

TIM McNEESE

INTRODUCTION BY
CASPAR W. WEINBERGER

CHELSEA HOUSE
P U B L I S H E R S
A Haights Cross Communications Company
Philadelphia

FRONTIS: The Battle of the Bulge, the final major German offensive of World War II, was so named because this military action that took place in the Ardennes forest caused the western war front to "bulge" toward France.

CHELSEA HOUSE PUBLISHERS

VP, PRODUCT DEVELOPMENT Sally Cheney
DIRECTOR OF PRODUCTION Kim Shinners
CREATIVE MANAGER Takeshi Takahashi
MANUFACTURING MANAGER Diann Grasse

STAFF FOR BATTLE OF THE BULGE

EXECUTIVE EDITOR Lee Marcott
PRODUCTION ASSISTANT Megan Emery
PICTURE RESEARCHER Noelle Nardone
SERIES & COVER DESIGNER Takeshi Takahashi
LAYOUT 21st Century Publishing and Communications, Inc.

©2004 by Chelsea House Publishers, a subsidiary of Haights Cross Communications. All rights reserved. Printed in China.

A Haights Cross Communications ✈ Company

http://www.chelseahouse.com

First Printing

1 3 5 7 9 8 6 4 2

Library of Congress Cataloging-in-Publication Data applied for.

ISBN 0-7910-7435 HC 0-7910-7794-2 PB

TABLE OF **CONTENTS**

INTRODUCTION

by Caspar W. Weinberger

There are many ways to study and teach history, which has perhaps been best defined as the "recording and interpretation of past events." Concentration can be on a compilation of major events, or on those events that help prove a theory of the author's. Or the "great man" theory can be applied to write the history of a country or an era, based on a study of the principal leaders or accepted geniuses who are felt to have shaped events that became part of the tapestry of history.

This new Chelsea House series adopts and continues the plan of studying six of the major battles and turning points of wars that did indeed shape much of the history of the periods before, during, and after those wars. By studying the events leading up to major battles and their results, inescapably one learns a great deal about the history of that period.

The first battle, chosen appropriately enough, is the Battle of Actium. There, in 31 B.C., the naval forces of Antony and Cleopatra, and those of Octavian, did battle off the northwest coast of Greece for control of the Roman world. Octavian's victory ended the Roman civil war and gave him unchallenged supremacy, leading to his designation as Augustus, Rome's first emperor. It is highly appropriate that the Battle of Actium be studied first for this series, because the battle was for many decades used as the starting point for a new era.

Next, in chronological order, is a study of the long years of battles between the forces of Richard the Lionhearted and Saladin. This Third Crusade, during the twelfth century, and the various military struggles for Acre and Jerusalem, was the background against which much of the history of modern Britain and Europe and the Middle East was played out.

Coming down to modern times, the series includes a study of the battle that forever changed naval warfare. This battle, the first between two ironclad warships, the *Monitor* and the *Merrimack*, ended the era of naval wars fought by great fleets of sail- or oar-powered ships, with their highly intricate maneuvers. After the *Monitor* and *Merrimack*, all naval battles became floating artillery duels with wholly different tactics and skills required.

The sinking of the German ship *Bismarck* during World War II was not so much a battle as a clear demonstration of the fact that a huge preponderance of naval force on one side could hunt down and destroy one of the most powerful battleships then afloat.

The continued importance of infantry warfare was demonstrated in the Battle of the Bulge, the final attempt of the German army, near the end of World War II, to stave off what in hindsight is now seen as the inevitable victory of the Allies.

The last battle in this series covers the Korean War—one of the most difficult and costly we have fought, and yet a war whose full story is very nearly forgotten by historians and teachers. The story of the Korean War embodies far more than simply the history of a war we fought in the 1950s. It is a history that is dominated by General Douglas MacArthur—but it is also a history of many of the foundation stores of American foreign and domestic policy in the past half century.

These six battles, and the wars of which they were a part, are well worth studying because, although they obviously cannot recount all of history from Actium to Korea, they can and do show the reader the similarities of many of those issues that drive people and governments to war. They also recount the development and changes in technologies by which people have acquired the ability to destroy their fellow creatures ever more effectively and completely.

With the invention and deployment of each new instrument of destruction, from the catapults that were capable of blasting great holes in the walls defending castles and forts, to today's nuclear weapons, the prediction has always been made that the effects and capability of each of those engines of destruction were so awful that their very availability would end war entirely. Thus far, those predictions have always been wrong, although as the full potential of nuclear weapons of mass destruction is increasingly better understood, it may well be that the very nature of these ultimate weapons will, indeed, mean that they will ever be used. However, the sheer numbers of these ultimate weapons possessed by many countries, and the possibilities of some of those countries falling under the dictatorship of some of the world's most dangerous leaders, combine to make imaginable a war that could indeed end the world. That is why the United States has expended so much to try to prevent countries such as Iraq and North Korea from continuing to be led by men as inherently dangerous as Saddam Hussein and Kim Sung Il, who are determined to acquire the world's most dangerous weapons.

An increasing knowledge of some of the great battles of the past that have so influenced history is essential unless we want to fulfill the old adage that those who forget history are likely to be condemned to repeat it — with all of its mistakes.

This old adage reminds us also that history is a study not just of great military victories, but also the story of battles lost and the many mistakes that were made by even the greatest of commanders.

After every engagement that involves American troops in action, even on a very small scale, the Pentagon conducts a "Lessons Learned" exercise. What went wrong? What should have been done differently? Did we need more troops, more artillery, more planes? Most important, could more lives of our own troops have been saved?

These mistakes or command errors are not only carefully studied and written about, but they form the basis for war games or exercises in which actual battle situations are re-fought—sometimes on paper—but frequently with troops re-enacting various parts of the combat action. These "lessons learned" exercises become a valuable part of the training of troops and are an even more valuable part of the training of leaders and commanders.

As we can all guess from the short discussions of some of those great battles in this series, there were many opportunities for different commanders and different plans to be used. Indeed, history is perhaps our greatest teacher, and a study of great battles is a great way to learn, even though each battle is different and there will be different lessons to be learned from the post-battle studies.

So, this Chelsea House series serves as a splendid beginning to our study of military history—a history that we must master if we want to see the expansion and success of our basic policy of maintaining peace with freedom.

It is not enough to consider threats to our security and our freedom. We must also be constantly ready to defend our freedom by keeping our ability to prevent any of those threats against us from materializing into real dangers. The study of great battles and how they were won, despite mistakes that have been made, is a vital part of our ability to keep peace with freedom.

BY: Caspar W. Weinberger
Chairman, FORBES Inc.
March 2003

Caspar W. Weinberger was the fifteenth U.S. secretary of defense, serving under President Ronald Reagan from 1981 to 1987.

Introduction

For three days, despite freezing temperatures and heavy fog, the Germans had advanced across the hill country—a ground bristling with tall, dark forests—of the Ardennes in France. They had swept by the thousands past the thinly protected American defense perimeter, catching whole battalions by surprise and capturing thousands of American government, or general-issue, soldiers (GIs) as prisoners on the first day of Hitler's grand plan to turn the war around in favor of the German Fatherland. It was to be his last great offensive, code-named "Watch on the Rhine."

Forming the German offensive's spearhead was a fearsome tank unit, the 1st stormtrooper (SS) *Panzer* (tank) division, moving as part of the *Wehrmacht*'s (war machine's) 6th Panzer army.

Leading the ferocious pack of German tanks was 29-year-old Lieutenant Colonel Jochen Peiper. Ruthless on the field of battle, Peiper had already seen action on the Russian front far to the east. Known as an aggressive, cold-blooded tank commander, he was as single-minded as any other German trooper in the opening days of the Ardennes Offensive. He intended to achieve the goals his *führer* (leader), Adolf Hitler, had laid out for the desperate German attack plan: Push across the Ardennes forest, destroy American pockets of resistance, cross the Meuse River on the west side of the Ardennes, and reach the Belgian city of Antwerp. The future of Germany, Hitler had assured his commanders, lay in the hands of such intrepid tank commanders as Lieutenant Colonel Peiper.

Despite his best efforts, Peiper had been unable to break through American positions in the middle of the Ardennes. After more than 72 hours, though, he had reached the small town of Stoumont, northwest of the strategic Ardennes crossroads of St. Vith. Here he overwhelmed a battalion of the U.S. 30th division, knocking out ten American tanks. At last, he had achieved his breakout. He had passed through the eastern half of the Ardennes and was making tracks toward the Meuse. U.S. infantrymen panicked, and fled the field to the west toward the safety of additional American forces.

A few miles ahead, word reached an American commander, Captain Berry of the 740th tank battalion, that Peiper had broken out at Stoumont. Immediately, he ordered his 14 tanks toward the small town. His tanks had already seen combat and had just been repaired. Berry was not even certain that they were working properly. He was uncertain if the radios even worked. New guns had also just been installed, and he had not had an opportunity to see if they were ready for battle.

As Berry's tank battalion rolled forward through the

winter sleet and fog on a course for the Stoumont railroad depot, he met other American tanks headed in the opposite direction. One retreating tank officer shouted as he passed Berry, "We're low on ammo and fuel!"

"And guts," Berry said to himself.

If Peiper was to be stopped at Stoumont, it was now up to Captain Berry's battalion. Discovering that his radios were nonfunctional, the American captain used hand signals to give instructions to his tank commanders. He ordered Lieutenant Powers to place his five tanks at the head of the armored column.

Suddenly, through the fog, Powers spotted the enemy ahead as a German Panther tank held its position at the curve of the road just 150 yards (137 meters) in the distance. Powers managed to fire on the Panther, hitting the Germans' gun mantlet, the shell ricocheting off. The shot still had killed the driver and the bow gunner. Then, the Panther lit up, its fuel bursting into flames.

Uncertain of what lay around the curve, Powers edged forward until a second German tank appeared. Again, Powers managed to get off the first round, which struck the German Tiger tank on its front slope plate, but the shell merely bounced off and caused little damage. A short two-tank battle followed until Powers's gun locked up. Quickly, the American lieutenant signaled a tank destroyer to move up. The Tiger blasted off two shells just as the 90-mm (3.5-inch) gun on the tank destroyer roared to life, leaving the menacing Tiger in flames.

Just then, Powers was able to unjam his tank gun, only to roll forward and spot a third enemy tank, a Panther, which Powers hit with a single shot that blew the German armored vehicle's muzzle off. Again, another enemy tank burst into flames. The fight was solidly in American hands as the remaining Wehrmacht tanks turned about and made tracks up a steep embankment toward

Stoumont, where they took positions behind the walls of a stone sanatorium.

The tanks of Captain Berry and Lieutenant Powers had thwarted the armored advance of General Peiper. The SS tank commander's breakout at Stoumont had failed, but the aggressive Nazi general believed his setback was only temporary. There were other roads, other towns, other opportunities to push past the American defenders of the Ardennes. The fight for the Ardennes, a Herculean struggle of mechanized warfare that the Americans would soon be calling the "Battle of the Bulge," had only just begun.

Adolf Hitler, a hero to the German people when this photograph was taken in 1937, began invading nearby countries by 1939. He was ultimately responsible for the deaths of millions across Europe.

An Expanding Global Conflict

During the decade preceding this final major German offensive of World War II, Europe had pursued a course of events leading to inevitable war. Throughout much of the 1930s, most industrialized nations experienced an economic downturn, a serious depression that made the people of some suffering countries vulnerable to political extremists who promised immediate answers to their financial woes. One such politician was the leader of a political organization called the National Socialist German Workers' (Nazi) Party—a psychopathic megalomaniac named Adolf Hitler.

Germany had been defeated during an earlier European conflict called the Great War (1914–1918). In time, it would be known as

World War I. The harsh peace treaty that ended the war utterly humiliated Germany's people, military, and leaders. As Germany chaffed under the Treaty of Versailles, men such as Adolf Hitler began plotting their personal and political revenge. The tenor of the times made Hitler's task of promoting political extremism an easy one. During the 1920s, Germany experienced the effects of a downward-spiraling postwar economy. Unemployment was rampant, and hyperinflation ate up a worker's wages.

The economic chaos left many desperate Germans open to the rabid racism and right-wing extremism of Adolf Hitler's Nazi Party and its propaganda. In one of his speeches, Hitler made clear his goals for the future of Germany: "I am going to fulfill the vow I made to myself: to know neither rest nor peace . . . until on the ruins of the wretched Germany of today there should have arisen once more a Germany of power and greatness, of freedom and splendor."[1]

As Hitler became more popular during the late 1920s and early 1930s, he was able to gain political influence. By 1929, his Nazi Party was the most significant minority political group in Germany. When the Great Depression caused the collapse of the German economy in 1930, Hitler was on the scene, offering answers, pointing the finger of blame at Jewish bankers, American capitalists, and Russian Communists.

By 1932, Hitler's National Socialists, with 800,000 members, had become the most powerful political organization in Germany. The elections held that summer resulted in the Nazi Party's gaining a majority of seats in the German legislature. Hitler, holding the majority support, was able to have himself selected by the aging German president, Paul von Hindenburg, as Germany's chancellor, a role similar to that of a prime minister. By January 30, 1933, Adolf Hitler was the number-two man in all of Germany.

In short order, the doddering Hindenburg was pushed aside, giving Hitler control of the government. When the old president died in August 1934, the office of Reich president was abolished, making Hitler the undisputed leader. He immediately began pursuing a course of rebuilding the dignity and pride of Germany by bringing its military back to life despite the prohibitions place on Germany by the Treaty of Versailles. As he developed his nation's military capabilities, he drew the attention of the Allied victors of World War I. Weak protests from France and Great Britain meant nothing to Hitler.

From the rise of Hitler as chancellor in 1933 until the opening days of World War II in 1939, Hitler increased his power base. He ignored the Versailles Treaty and ordered his armies into the German Rhineland, the western lands of his country that bordered France, in 1936. As Hitler calculated his next steps, he was certain Great Britain and France would not take bold measures to stop him, as long as "their interests were not directly threatened." As for the United States, that distant democracy "worried Hitler not at all."[2]

Hitler's political extremism was not the only challenge facing the democracies of the West during the 1930s. In 1921, an Italian Socialist, Benito Mussolini, had founded the Fascist Party, a group that espoused strong antidemocratic ideas and intended to take control of the Italian government. In Japan, military leaders took control of the government of their nation and began marching against their neighbors.

Hitler and Mussolini became partners in extremism when they formed an alliance in October 1936. The alliance, called the Rome-Berlin Axis, foresaw a future world that was destined to revolve around their own political philosophies after being forced into submission by their powerful military war machines. The following month, Germany and Japan signed the Anti-Comintern Pact, as both nations agreed to fight the spread of communism. Although they were disturbed by the spread of right-wing extremism, fascism, and Nazism, the leaders of the democratic states took no action to stop it.

During the fall of 1938, Hitler took another decisive act of aggression as he threatened to march to the east and occupy the western perimeter lands of neighboring Czechoslovakia, called the Sudetenland. By March 1939, Hitler's army stormed across the border into Czechoslovakia and occupied the Czech lands of historic Bohemia and Moravia.

Each bold step taken by Hitler as the leader of a newly militarized Germany had been done with a calculated risk. He pushed his enemies, invaded their territory, and bullied the Western democracies without a thought of ever going too far. He was bound on a course for war. His thrust to the east—including Austria, the Sudetenland, and now Czechoslovakia—made his next target clear: Poland. Since Poland shared a border with the Soviet Union, the governments of Great Britain and France turned to the Soviets for aid in organizing an effort to stop the ever-expanding German war machine. The Soviet leader, Joseph Stalin, was in no mood to join forces with the Western democracies, however. On August 23, 1939, the German and Soviet governments signed a nonaggression pact in Moscow, one that called for dividing Poland between the two nations.

With an assurance that the Soviets would not consider an attack on Poland as an act of aggression, but merely as an opportunity to divide the spoils, Hitler ordered his troops, planes, and tanks across the Polish border on September 1, 1939. The date marks the opening of the hostilities that became World War II. The attack came at 4:45 A.M. as 250,000 German troops in 60 divisions marched, drove, and flew across the border. Cities and towns were utterly destroyed in the face of the Nazi *blitzkrieg*, or "lightning war." The Polish army was no match for the modern, highly mechanized forces of the Germans. In fact, among the Polish forces that met Hitler's mobilized invasion were cavalrymen on horseback carrying lances.

Such blatant aggression drew an immediate response

Nazi soldiers targeted snipers in Warsaw, Poland, during the German invasion in September 1939. Poland's antiquated military forces were no match for the efficient "blitzkrieg" strikes.

from France and Great Britain, and two days later, both nations declared war on Germany, each gearing into full military mobilization. Within two weeks, the Soviet Union, at the invitation of the German government, invaded Poland from the east. The reluctant warrior nations of France and Great Britain did not move against Germany immediately, however. Throughout the winter of 1939–1940, the Western powers remained largely immobile and the war was derisively referred to not as blitzkrieg, but as "Sitzkrieg."

Despite almost immediate declarations of war from France and England, neither side moved offensively for months, leaving both Germany and the Soviet Union to engage in additional invasions against their neighbors. In November, after fruitless negotiations demanding a Finnish surrender, the Soviets sent planes against Helsinki and other cities in Finland. When spring arrived across Europe, the Germans began a series of lightning-quick and successful invasions against a long list of Western European powers, including France and Great Britain. That April, blitzkrieg attacks struck Denmark and Norway.

Then Hitler launched a series of massive assaults against the Netherlands, Belgium, and Luxembourg. With military efficiency, German tanks rolled through these small, relatively defenseless states and headed straight toward France itself. Behind them were 75 German divisions. French defense lines fell apart in the wake of the German juggernaut offensive, splitting the Allied forces and trapping some French troops and the entire British army along the coastal reaches of Dunkirk. By the skin of their teeth, the British were able to evacuate nearly one-third of a million men, mostly British forces, from their precarious toehold on the French coast to the relative safety of the British Isles.

Three weeks later, the entire French military surrendered, unable to meet the immediate challenge of dozens of infantry divisions, plus *Luftwaffe* (German air force) support. The French government toppled on June 22, 1940, facing the presence of German forces occupying three-fifths of the country. From August through September, the air forces of the British and the Germans shot it out in the skies over the English Channel. Holding out against the German air onslaught required nearly every available resource Great Britain had at its disposal. Hundreds of small yet maneuverable British air fighters, the famous Spitfires, flew rings around the heavier yet deadly German *Messerschmitts*. By the end of September, Hitler called off his air offensive, having suffered serious losses among his Luftwaffe forces. When the air war over England ended, the Germans had lost just short of 2,700 planes while the British lost just over 900.

It was a singular triumph for the people of Great Britain and for Prime Minister Winston Churchill. With the failure of Germany's Operation Sea Lion, and a defiant Great

Britain still intact, the stage was set for the ultimate defeat of Hitler's forces. By the fall of 1941, however, the end of the war was not even close. Other nations, including the Soviet Union and the United States, had yet to join the conflict.

With the failure of the German Luftwaffe to bring the people of the British Isles to their knees, Hitler soon changed his strategy, turning toward the Mediterranean Sea where he intended to launch attacks against Egypt and the crucial Suez Canal. Here, he hoped to close off the Mediterranean to the British, in effect by cutting off their oil supply through the canal. He also made plans to attack the Soviet Union first, regardless of any nonaggression treaty he had made with the Soviet leader, Joseph Stalin.

The attack against the Soviet Union did not take place until June 22, 1941, a date remembered for the fall of France just one year earlier. The German attack on the Soviet Union stretched across an 1,800-mile-long (3,334-kilometer-long) front. Soviet resistance was sporadic, and in some cases, completely lacking. Only the early snows of a Russian winter saved the Soviet Union from utter destruction. Before the end of December 1941, the Soviet command regrouped and took the offensive, determined to remove the German menace from Soviet soil.

That same month, December 1941, witnessed the opening of hostilities and an expansion of World War II halfway across the globe. On the morning of December 7, Japanese air and naval forces struck in a surprise attack against U.S. naval and army installations on the Hawaiian island of Oahu. The Japanese assault on Pearl Harbor, which resulted in the deaths of 2,500 Americans, drew the United States into World War II when President Franklin Roosevelt (FDR) requested, on the following day, a declaration of war against Japan. Yet even as the American resolve for war was focused on the Japanese, Adolf Hitler performed one of the greatest blunders of his military and political career. Just three days following the attack on Pearl Harbor, Hitler declared war on the United States. Now, two great powers—Roosevelt's United States and Stalin's Communist Soviet Union—were allied against one common enemy.

The Grand Alliance (the newly allied countries of Great Britain, the Soviet Union, and the United States) was now at war with the Axis powers of Germany, Italy, and Japan. Throughout the first nine months of 1942, the Allies faced grim news at nearly every turn. German submarines prowled the high seas and sank nearly 700 Allied ships between January and July. That fall, Hitler launched a massive campaign across the Soviet Union, bound for the Soviet oil fields of the Caucasus in the region between the Black and Caspian seas. By autumn, the Germans were laying siege to the Russian city of Stalingrad. The siege dragged on throughout the remainder of the year as the German 6th army tightened its control over the beleaguered city on the Volga River. That spring and summer, German tank and infantry forces in North Africa were continuing to advance across the desert regions, finally breaking through the British defenses in Egypt, bound straight for Alexandria. Hitler's *Afrika Korps* appeared unstoppable.

The final months of 1942 brought significant events that turned the tide of war in favor of the Allies. Panzer General Erwin Rommel's tanks were finally halted at El Alamein on the Mediterranean Sea in northwestern Egypt in early November. By November, the Germans were wedged between the advancing British tanks from the east and a joint force of American and British paratroopers who landed along the coasts of Morocco and Algeria, catching the Nazis in a pincer movement. On November 12, British forces captured the Libyan port of Tobruk, and by May 1943, the city of Tunis fell to the Allies, removing the last remnants of Nazi resistance along the southern shores of the Mediterranean.

A German tank crew near ruined buildings in Stalingrad, Russia, part of the 1942–1943 siege on that city. Three hundred thousand Nazis finally surrendered. The war caused lasting animosity between Germans and Russians, even in peacetime.

As 1943 opened, the Allies were gaining ground on nearly every front. The war had turned almost completely in their favor as the Americans took a greater role with each passing month of combat. That year the Germans lost Africa, their presence in the Mediterranean was reduced, and Mussolini's government collapsed. British and American forces invaded across the Mediterranean, landing on the island of Sicily and using the triangular-shaped island as a springboard to invade and liberate Italy. In the meantime, Stalingrad had held against the Germans and the Soviets had pulled off an effective counteroffensive, trapping the German 6th army inside the city. Three hundred thousand Germans surrendered at Stalingrad in February 1943. As Soviet armies drove the remnant of German resistance from their country, the end of the war seemed determined. Even so, there would be two more years of fighting in Europe.

American soldiers disembarked on June 6, 1944, during the Allied landing at Normandy on the northwestern coast of France. D day was the beginning of the long-delayed second European front.

From Normandy to the Ardennes

When the three leaders of the Grand Alliance—Churchill, Roosevelt, and Stalin—met at a conference in Teheran, Iran, in the latter days of November 1943, the outcome of World War II was certain. The Allies would win the war and Hitler's dream of a German Empire that would last 1,000 years would die. There were serious obstacles that lay ahead, though, for any complete Allied victory. At the conference, Stalin was adamant about establishing the long-delayed second European front. Already in the planning, President Roosevelt promised Stalin that the front would be established within six months of the conference. As Roosevelt promised, the front became reality the following June.

The planned Allied landing along the French coast at Normandy was code-named "Operation Overlord." American General Dwight D. Eisenhower had been planning the details of the invasion since the fall of 1943. When the invasion was launched on June 6, 1944, remembered in history as D day, the Allies landed five assault divisions on France's Normandy beaches under the guns of a strong, determined German opposition. During the ten days of fighting following D day, Allied forces advanced in the face of heavy German resistance while taking many casualties. The Germans fought so tenaciously that the Allies were only able to gain a few yards of ground daily; but while progress was slow, it was steady. Within three months of D day, the Allies had succeeded in landing more than 2 million men and close to half a million vehicles, including tanks, along the barren coastlands of northern France.

During the six months that followed, the Germans fought doggedly to retain their hold on Western Europe. By August, the Allies—largely British, American, and Canadian forces—had liberated the French capital of Paris. The Germans continued losing ground at every turn, yet Germany continued to fight.

As the liberators of Normandy advanced, the Germans they faced were largely combat veterans; many of their officers had fought along the Russian front and they were well armed and tenacious. On July 11, a Panzer division was able to turn and launch a major counterattack but the 9th and 30th U.S. infantry divisions pushed back hard, forcing the Germans to suffer a 25 percent casualty rate. As the weeks of fighting mounted, the Germans ran short of artillery shells and medicine. According to author Stephen Ambrose, these frontline troops knew they had to hold their positions, for, if the Americans were able to advance far enough "there was nothing between them and the German border." This ensured that, with each passing day, "the Germans dug even deeper, fought even harder."[3]

On July 31, the Americans broke out of their Normandy beachheads at Avranches after seven weeks of fighting. Hitler's immediate response to the news was one of despondence and depression; all appeared lost to him. The Soviets were advancing from the east through the Balkans and other Eastern European states and the Allies were pushing up from southern France and Italy. His Nazi-controlled German Empire seemed to be headed toward defeat. Despite the difficulties facing him by September 16, however, Hitler called a special meeting with his inner council of generals at his headquarters at the Wolf's Lair, hidden in the forests of East Prussia. Four high-ranking officers were present—Field Marshal Wilhelm Keitel, supreme commander of all German armies; Colonel General Alfred Jodl, chief of operations; the legendary Panzer commander and veteran of the Russian front, General Heinz Guderian; and General Kreipe, a representative of air marshal Hermann Göring, head of the German Luftwaffe.

General Jodl opened the meeting, as he typically did, by reporting on the state of the German military. Much of his news was negative; Jodl described the difficulties of the fighting in France, especially in the region of the Ardennes, where some of the hardest fighting of World War I had been done nearly 30 years earlier. Suddenly, in the middle of Jodl's presentation, Hitler, who had appeared distracted, depressed, almost lifeless, raised his hand suddenly and ordered Jodl to stop. For the next two minutes, no one— not even Hitler—said a word. Then, the führer finally spoke, his face flushed with life, "his eyes luminous, the signs of care and sickness gone."[4] He blurted out his plan for meeting the challenge of the Americans on the Western front: "I have made a momentous decision. I am taking the offensive. Here—out of the Ardennes! Across the Meuse [River] and on to Antwerp!"[5] Even to the gathered officers, some of whom had become accustomed to erratic outbursts from the leader, Hitler's announcement was shocking.

Everything his generals had learned from their military schooling and years of field experience told them that the Wehrmacht should, given their defeats at Normandy and across France, continue to fight while gradually retreating back to the Rhine River, located along the German border, to make a stand to defend their own country. Now, here was Hitler, untrained in the military arts and a leader who despised being on the defensive, ordering a massive strike against his enemies, a strategy unformed and unclear in its details, yet one he was certain constituted a move of genius. When General Field Marshal Gerd von Rundstedt, the commander of all German forces in the Western theater received word of Hitler's intentions, he was shocked:

> When I was first told about the proposed offensive in the Ardennes, I protested against it as vigorously as I could. The forces at our disposal were much, much too weak for such far-reaching objectives. It was only up to one to obey. It was a nonsensical operation, and the most stupid part of it was the setting of Antwerp as the target. If we reached the Meuse [River] we should have got down on our knees and thanked God—let alone try to reach Antwerp.[6]

Yet even as various German commanders learned of Hitler's plan, one that made them instantly skeptical of its potential success, the German leader had already determined it was brilliant. He had a name for the offensive—*Wacht am Rhein* (Watch on the Rhine)—which he had borrowed from an old patriotic German song. When it succeeded, as Hitler was certain it would, the result would be a complete turnaround for the war. Germany would again determine the course of the war and the Allies would experience, in the führer's words, "a new Dunkirk!"[7]

Hitler and his commanders, Deile, Jodl, Raeder, and Brauchitsch, planned the ambitious counteroffensive, nicknamed "Watch on the Rhine," in the Ardennes forest. Hitler's officers initially considered it a foolish strategy.

The next day, Hitler ordered his commanders to begin making preparations for a counteroffensive. Jodl was to create the overall plan. Though he was not personally convinced Hitler's dream of a successful winter offensive would succeed, he realized that the military had few options. With multiple Allied armies driving hard toward Berlin, Jodl accepted that "given our desperate situation, we must not shrink from staking everything on one card."[8] Keitel was to determine the logistical necessities: how much gasoline, how many supplies, what types and amounts of ammunition. Hitler himself ordered five Panzer divisions to be delivered to the region west of Cologne, Germany, where they would be prepared for the counteroffensive. At the center of his plan he appointed General Rudolf Gercke as the commander of the 6th Panzer army. Gercke would play a considerable role in the planned offensive.

Within two weeks of Hitler's decision to launch an offensive, much of the planning work had been accomplished. Special plans had been developed to deliver tanks across the Rhine River into French territory. Ferries were refitted so they could carry locomotives and the King Tiger tanks, each weighing 70 tons (71 metric tons). Ammunition dumps and supply depots were established east of the Rhine. Gercke spent much of his time equipping the trains of the German state railways, the *Reichsbahn*, with armor-plated locomotives and antiaircraft guns mounted on special railroad cars.

By October 11, Jodl presented a version of his planned Ardennes Offensive to Hitler. Code-named "Christrose," the plan centered on the deployment of three major army groups—the 6th Panzer army, the 5th Panzer army, and the 7th army. Between these three armies, 30 divisions were included—18 infantry and 12 tank. Jodl's plan was a deceptively simple one, straightforward and tightly drawn. It called for the unleashing of a wide front sent forward suddenly, surprising the enemy. Within a day, the offensive was to reach the Meuse River. By the end of one week, the armies were to reach the city of Antwerp in Belgium. In its wake, the great German offensive was to annihilate 30 Anglo-American divisions, crushing those that had broken the Germans during the summer fighting at Normandy. The plan, which included everything the führer had wanted, was satisfactory to Hitler.

By October 27, however, alternate plans that were both more realistic and scaled back in their goals, were presented to the German leader in an attempt to make Hitler understand that his grand goal of destroying the Allies in the west and marching his forces to Belgian Antwerp was not feasible. Developed by General Field Marshals Rundstedt and Walther Model, the revamped plans—called the "Small Solution"—focused largely on the annihilation of the U.S. 1st army, which had been advancing east since Normandy and represented the greatest immediate threat to the Germans. Neither plan was acceptable to Hitler, who referred to both plans as "incapable of producing decisive results."[9] The plan to destroy 30 Allied divisions and capture Antwerp remained intact. Although Model was selected by Hitler to lead the Ardennes Offensive, Model did not think the drive through the Ardennes would succeed. He noted with frustration and resignation: "This damned thing hasn't got a leg to stand on!"[10] As for Rundstedt, he stated his firm belief that "all, absolutely all conditions for the possible success of such an offensive were lacking."[11]

Although Hitler and many of his generals did not see eye-to-eye on the proposed offensive plan, they all agreed on one thing: The plan must remain secret. The element of surprise was crucial to the opening of the offensive, which was reliant on catching the Allies off-guard.

As Hitler's generals planned the details of the secret counteroffensive, the Nazi leader was planning some additional details beyond the skeletal proposal he had originally envisioned. On October 21, he summoned to his headquarters at Wolf's Lair an SS major of near-legendary status and a favorite commando of Hitler's, Otto Skorzeny.

A fellow Austrian, Skorzeny had been recruited to the Nazi cause at age 24. He was, in Hitler's mind, the perfect Aryan, a giant of a man standing well over six feet tall with a massive frame. Skorzeny was a product of Prussian military school and sported a jagged scar across his left cheek, from the ear to the mouth, which he had received during a rapier duel as a student in Vienna. (He and his opponent were fighting over a female ballet dancer.) He was highly intelligent and drew respect from colleagues and enemies alike. To British intelligence, this daring commando had become known as "the most dangerous man in Europe."[12]

Hitler explained why he had summoned the extraordinary commando. "Stay awhile," said the Nazi leader, with

German commando Otto Skorzeny was personally charged by Hitler with the task of selecting and training a brigade to infiltrate enemy lines and sabotage key military and transport targets.

excitement in his voice. "I am now going to give you the most important job of your life. In December, Germany will start a great offensive. It may decide her fate."[13] He filled Skorzeny in on the details of the planned Ardennes counter-offensive and then revealed the role he wanted the Aryan commando to play. Skorzeny and a brigade of his selection were to train to move behind enemy lines during the

German offensive, disguised in American and British uniforms, while driving Allied vehicles such as tanks and jeeps. These disguised commandos were to pass themselves off as Allied troops, while causing as much chaos as possible. They were to "seize bridges over the Meuse, spread rumors, give false orders, breed confusion and panic." Skorzeny accepted the clandestine mission, code-named "Operation Grief." "I'm giving you unlimited power to set up your brigade," assured Hitler. "Use it, Colonel!" With that sentence, the German leader had advanced Skorzeny in rank, bringing a smile to the seasoned commando's face.[14]

"Operation Grief" Compromised

Skorzeny had been given his assignment on October 22, nearly two months before the opening of the counteroffensive. Just four days later, an unfortunate communication was sent across the entire German Western front, which Skorzeny felt completely jeopardized his mission. On October 26, copies of a Wehrmacht notice were distributed which included the words "Secret Commando Operations" at the top of the page, along with the following announcement: "The Führer has ordered the formation of a special unit of approximately two battalion strength for use on the Western Front in special operations. . . ."* The communication continued by requesting any German soldier who could speak English to volunteer to participate in Skorzeny's clandestine "Operation Grief."

When word of the announcement reached the Austrian commando, Skorzeny was shocked and furious. He was certain the paper would fall into the hands of Allied intelligence, yet Hitler convinced Skorzeny to stick to his mission.

As for Skorzeny's concerns that security had been breached by the front-line communiqué, he need not have worried. Allied intelligence did, in fact, gain knowledge of the widely disseminated document by early November. The paper was deemed a hoax, however, nothing more than a piece of German propaganda designed to spread fear and anxiety through the American units assigned to the Ardennes.

* Quoted in Danny S. Parker, *Battle of the Bulge: Hitler's Ardennes Offensive, 1944–1945.* Conshohocken, PA: Combined Publishing, 1991, p. 170.

"Watch on
the Rhine"

Members of the U.S. 1st army used white clothing, or "snow capes," as camouflage to fight in snow-covered Europe during December 1944. Allied forces knew the German offensive would be launched sometime that winter, but did not know where.

Throughout the following weeks, from the last week of October through mid-December, deployment of the needed troops, equipment, fuel, and supplies for the bold Ardennes counteroffensive went on. The original opening date for the offensive was set by Hitler for late November but he agreed to change the date several times, moving it to December 10, then to the twelfth, then the fifteenth. A final change moved the launch date to December 16. The circle of generals, commanders, and chiefs-of-staff at corps level had to be widened as the date for the offensive drew nearer, and the utmost precautions were taken to continue the veil of secrecy surrounding Hitler's plans. Historian John Toland described the extensive efforts taken to keep the rapidly approaching German strike date secret:

> To guarantee security, generals were ordered to draft their own maps, take care of their own secretarial work, and keep all secret material on their persons day and night. Radio operators sent coded messages to fictitious headquarters, fictitious messages to genuine head-quarters, genuine messages to headquarters a hundred miles [161 kilometers] from their advertised locations. False rumors were spread in lower echelons, in bars, in restaurants for the ears of Allied agents.[15]

Even as the Wehrmacht continued its plans for the December offensive, the Allied armies of the British and Americans did not stand idly by. Their advance across France and Belgium had continued since the first landings on the beaches of Normandy back in June. As early as late August, five different Allied armies moving in relatively coordinated fashion had crossed the French river Seine, then continued their hot pursuit of ever-retreating German forces. These advancing armies included General Bernard Montgomery's 21st army group, the U.S. 1st army, and the U.S. 3rd army, under the direct command of General George Patton.

By mid-August, only the German 19th army was still operating in southern France. As described in Trevor Nevitt Dupuy's book, when the last German resistance in the south finally fell, the Wehrmacht losses in that region had mounted to close to 100,000. On August 28, the U.S. 3rd infantry division captured 15,000 German prisoners near the Rhône River, and this portion of the Allied advance resulted in a seven-mile-long (11-kilometer-long) stretch of road littered with "dead men, dead horses and wrecked vehicles."[16] By September 11, General Patton's 3rd army's right flank met up with American and French units that had landed in southern France early that summer. This joining of forces completed a long Allied offensive line stretching north from Switzerland across eastern France, through the Ardennes, past the German city of Aachen (home of the ninth-century Frankish King Charlemagne), then west to the English Channel, reaching the Belgian city of Ostend.

The lengthy strides made by American, British, and Canadian forces through June, July, August, and September largely dried up by October and November. There was progress by the middle of November when Patton's tanks were rolling, after facing a severe fuel shortage, having crossed the Moselle River and captured Metz, a city in northeastern France, on November 22. This victory placed the Lorraine region, wedged historically between eastern France and western Germany, on the Allied side of the ledger. The 6th army group, which included the U.S. 7th army and the French 1st army, seized the German city of Strasbourg and pierced the defensive Siegfried Line. In the face of such Allied victories, Hitler felt even greater pressure to launch his Watch on the Rhine offensive by December.

The forested region Hitler had targeted for his planned offensive, the Ardennes, was hardly an easy ground for combat. Fighting had taken place there as early as the days of the Roman Empire, when the primeval Germanic forest was referred to in a military report as "a frightful place, full of terrors."[17] European leaders from Charlemagne to Napoleon had fought across its dark woods, and during World War I, the French commander, Field Marshal Ferdinand Foch, described the region succinctly: "It is impenetrable."[18]

It was the combination of typography and physiography that made the Ardennes so unlikely a place for a battle, especially in a century of increasingly mechanized warfare. Although not all of the Ardennes was forested, it was an extremely rough terrain. Heavy forests dotted the Ardennes landscape but so did cleared fields, deep valleys, hilly ridges, and "steep ravines [alternating] with heath, bogs, narrow winding trails and trackless woodland."[19] The region was cut across by a number of rivers and lesser streams. On a map, the small streams might appear easy to cross, but many of them had cut deep ravines and embankments, rendering them almost impassable, especially with heavy machines of war.

Hitler intended to drive his counteroffensive through two of the larger regions of the Ardennes—the Eifel

The Ardennes: No Place to Fight?

Even as Hitler and his high command hammered out their plan to launch a counteroffensive in the Ardennes forest, the Allies looked at the same ground and concluded that no one would choose to fight on such a field. During the fall of 1944, Eisenhower had some concern that he had forced Allied units to spread out too thinly and that the Ardennes was vulnerable to attack, its 88-mile-long (142-kilometer-long) front held by only three divisions.

Just to be certain, however, that the Ardennes represented no possibilities as a battleground for a possible German offensive, General Omar Bradley and General Troy Middleton, the commander of the U.S. 8th corps holding Bastogne, visited the wooded region in question and examined its possible threat. Driving through the Ardennes, both generals agreed that, throughout the region, "there was nothing within the Ardennes territory east of the Meuse River, a formidable obstacle, to constitute a worthwhile objective for a German attack."* At one point, Bradley stated his opinion to Middleton: "Don't worry, Troy. They won't come through here." Bradley provided Middleton with only one additional division to hold the Ardennes.

* *Source:* Quoted in John S. D. Eisenhower, *The Bitter Woods.* New York: G. P. Putnam's Sons, 1969, p. 101.

(a plateau region in northwestern Germany) and the Ardennes proper. The Eifel fit the description of the common view of the Ardennes: heavily wooded hill country on the German border, situated between the Rhine and Moselle rivers. Movement through this part of the Ardennes was tricky, but the heavy forest cover could hide an army from any airplanes scouting for their whereabouts. In fact, the Americans had captured much of this portion of the Ardennes during their late summer–early fall advances. The Eifel was also home to a number of German rail lines, many of which had been built for the armies of Kaiser William I during World War I. Although these rail systems could be used to move equipment and troops across the region, they moved along open fields, not forests, and were susceptible to aerial bombing.

The Ardennes proper was a wedge-shaped piece of real estate that spread over the borders of Luxembourg, Belgium, and northern France. This area ran to the Meuse River and was divided into three contiguous sub-compartments, including the High Ardennes (even this land was not that high, only standing approximately 2,500 feet (762 meters) above sea level), the Low Ardennes to the north, and a middle valley region known as the Famenne Depression. Thick timberland covered the High Ardennes, while the valley was nearly without any trees. An army could advance best through either the Famenne Depression or the Low Ardennes, but even then, the significant number of rivers, marshes, and deep gorges made any movement treacherous. Even roads were typically narrow, often clinging precariously to slopping hillsides and deep canyons.

The Ardennes were, prior to the war, almost uninhabited. The region had no cities, although several, including Liege and Luxembourg City, stood on the edges of the forested lands. Numerous small towns dotted the Ardennes landscape, most of them situated at crossroads. Their streets were narrow, their bridges made of medieval stone and hardly usable for weapons such as tanks, and the roads themselves were largely dirt that turned into heavy, thick mud when rain or snow fell.

A combination of factors, then, made a counteroffensive through the Ardennes in the dead of winter a long shot for the Wehrmacht at best and a nightmare at worst. Even Hitler's generals understood the difficulties inherent in this singular gamble. As the commander of the German 6th Panzer army, General Josef Dietrich, summed up:

> All [Hitler] wants me to do is cross a river, capture Brussels, then go on and take Antwerp! And all this in the worst time of the year through the Ardennes where the snow is waist deep and there isn't room to deploy four tanks abreast let alone armored divisions! Where it doesn't get light until eight and it's dark again at four and with reformed divisions made up chiefly of kids and sick old men—and at Christmas![20]

Despite the obvious dangers of the plan, Hitler could not be swayed. By December 7, 1944, just a week before the launch date for the Ardennes campaign, the Wehrmacht began moving tens of thousands of troops and their supplies as well as support vehicles toward the Ardennes. Nearly every train in the region was routed on a line toward the Ardennes, traveling at night to provide cover for the massive movements of men and material. Night after night, trains were loaded in the evening, delivered their loads to their destination, and returned back across the Rhine River by 3:00 A.M. By December 11, nearly everything and everyone included in the counteroffensive had been moved into position in the "Zone of the Offensive." That same week,

During the battle for the Ardennes, Nazi soldiers encountered rough terrain that seriously hampered troop and materiel movement. Train tracks installed by the Germans during World War I were again used to maneuver forces into place.

Hitler moved his headquarters outside a medieval castle in Ziegenberg, near Frankfurt, so he could direct the offensive near the front. It was from Ziegenberg that the Wehrmacht had successfully directed the Ardennes campaign of 1940.

On December 11, Hitler called a meeting of his top generals and field commanders in his bunker in Ziegenberg; approximately 60 officers were ordered to attend. Loaded onto buses, they were driven along a winding route to make certain none of them knew where he was once he arrived at the meeting site. Hitler's precautions concerning the secrecy of the soon-to-be-launched campaign and thwarting any possible assassination attempt had reached its threshold. Historian John S. D. Eisenhower described what followed:

> Before their departure from Ziegenberg Castle the generals were stripped of their weapons and briefcases, and when the bus stopped this normally proud group was led between a double row of SS storm troopers into a deep bunker, which turned out to be Hitler's command post, known as the [Eagle's Nest]. . . . Ushered into the meeting room, the generals were soon joined by Keitel, Jodl, and the Führer. It was a strange meeting, although strange meetings were far from unusual in Hitler's headquarters.[21]

They met in a room large enough for the 60 officers in attendance and an armed SS guard standing behind every commander's chair. Hitler sat at a long, narrow table with Keitel at his right and Jodl at his left. Many of those attending were combat-seasoned veterans and some present noted that Hitler did not look well, that he appeared "a broken man, with an unhealthy color, a caved-in appearance . . . with trembling hands . . . his body seemed still more decrepit and he was a man grown old."[22]

For two hours, Hitler spoke to his military leaders, reminding them of his past military successes and how the Allied coalition was becoming shaky. Knowing there were some present who doubted the possibilities of success for his planned Ardennes counteroffensive, Hitler offered many assurances. The Americans who occupied the Ardennes suspected nothing; he assured everyone that the German Luftwaffe would provide between 800 and 1,000 planes for air cover during the offensive; and all of the required heavy equipment and vehicles had been moved into place to launch the offensive. The troops were waiting, ready to fight, their morale high, and their equipment in perfect order; there would be plenty of gasoline, ammunition, and fighting spirit. Germany was therefore ready for a fight in the Ardennes. Hitler became extremely animated during his presentation, despite signs of his poor health, and filled the room with his continuing vision of a great Germany led by the National Socialist German Workers' Party.

Without question, a tremendous amount of planning had gone into the intended offensive. The plans called for coordination, hard-hitting movements, and, most crucial, the appropriate weather. The Watch on the Rhine had been planned down to the last detail. It would be launched at 5:30 A.M. on December 16. The massive forward movement would include three immense armies pushing through the rugged terrain of the Ardennes, their front stretching from Monschau in the north, along the Rur River to Echternach, 50 miles (81 kilometers) to the south, on the banks of the Sauer. Following a quick thrust through the Ardennes, these offensive armies would cross the Meuse River, between the northern city of Liege and the smaller town of Namur, situated to the southwest. Here, the advancing armies were to swing to the northwest, bypassing Brussels, Belgium, on their left flank, and head straight to the city of Antwerp. From the first day of the offensive until the triumphant arrival in Antwerp it would last less than seven days. The successful offensive would rock the Allied coalition; the British and Americans would be crushed and desperate to end the fighting by suing for a separate peace, leaving only the Soviets to face the fury of the German war machine.

At the meeting, Hitler announced the names of the armies and their commanders that would participate in the offensive. General Josef "Sepp" Dietrich, an early recruit to Nazism who had also served as Hitler's bodyguard, was assigned the command of the 6th Panzer army. The 5th Panzer army was to be led by Baron Hasso von Manteuffel, a 47-year-old veteran of the Russian campaigns. Finally, the 7th army, comprised largely of infantry, would advance under General Ernst Brandenberger.

The main line of attack was assigned to Dietrich, whose forces were to move along the offensive's northern flank. His troops were among the best assigned to the Watch on the Rhine. Many of them were *Waffen* (weapon) SS troops, elite German troops and diehard Nazis, who were culled from various units to create exactly the kind of determined fighting force Hitler needed to invade west. A significant number of them had fought on the Eastern front against tenacious Soviet troops. Dietrich's 6th Panzer army included four Panzer divisions and five infantry divisions; its line of assault was to engage the enemy from the jumping-off place at Monschau to the Losheim Gap, on to Elsenborn Ridge; then, after crossing the Meuse River, it would complete the drive to Antwerp.

The center of the German line of advance belonged to General Manteuffel and his 5th Panzer army. Manteuffel, known before the war for his pentathlon and equestrian skills, was descended from a long line of German military commanders. A favorite of Hitler's, he was assigned a pair of goals: Manteuffel was to bring two infantry divisions to bear on Allied forces centered in the Schnee Eifel salient, then seize the crossroads town of St. Vith. Here, at least six roads converged, as well as a major rail line. His remaining forces, including two additional infantry divisions and

General Sepp Dietrich visited Hitler's headquarters, the Eagle's Nest, outside of Frankfurt. Dietrich commanded the 6th Panzer division against the Allies and was given a choice assignment, the main line of attack along the northern flank.

three Panzer units, were to advance south of Schnee Eifel, through Luxembourg.

On Manteuffel's left flank, the 7th army was to advance under the command of Brandenberger. These troops were to capture the region between Vianden and Echternach to the south, a heavily wooded region with few good roads. While Brandenberger's advance was considered less vital than those of the 5th Panzer and 6th Panzer, it was assumed he would have to deal directly with any counterthrust launched by the Allied tank commander every German Panzer general respected—General Patton.

Once the assignments and expectations for each commander and his forces had been laid out by Hitler, the curious meeting at the Eagle's Nest was over. As the führer spoke his final words to his commanders, he made it clear how vital their success was to the future of his Third Reich and of Germany itself:

> This battle is to decide whether we shall live or die. I want all my soldiers to fight hard and without pity. The battle must be fought with brutality and all resistance must be broken in a wave of terror. In this most serious hour of the Fatherland, I expect every one of my soldiers to be courageous and again courageous. The enemy must be beaten—now or never! Thus lives our Germany![23]

Over the following days, the last efforts of preparation for the offensive were carried out: Tanks were moved forward and over the German defensive perimeter, the Siegfried Line; troops scattered layers of straw in front of the tanks to muffle the sounds of their treads; ammunition was moved forward; all radio traffic was halted; and special camouflage units were dispatched to each village where tanks and troops were gathered. German units also faced roll call half a dozen times a day, to ensure that no one had deserted and informed the unsuspecting enemy. Wehrmacht troops warmed themselves over charcoal fires, rather than wood, just to keep telltale drifts of smoke to a minimum.

The Germans had amassed more than 3 million gallons of gasoline and oil at the frontlines, with an additional 3 million promised in reserve. Every Panzer had a fuel supply adequate for 100 miles (161 kilometers) of advance. An eight-day supply of ammunition of more than 15,000 tons (15,241 metric tons) had been stockpiled, with an additional eight-day cache due to arrive soon. Nearly 400 Luftwaffe planes stood at the ready, including 80 newly designed aircraft that sported jet engines. On the night of December 15–16, 20 Wehrmacht divisions representing 250,000 combatants stood ready for the fight that would determine the future of Adolf Hitler's Germany.

The Nazi soldier was expected to have an almost fanatical devotion to his commander and to his führer, the leader of the German Fatherland.

Into the Woods

I n the early morning hours of December 16, a heavy fog hung across the landscape of the Schnee Eifel. The fog was a blessing to the assembled German troops; it would cover their forward movements during the opening hours of their planned attack. Hundreds of thousands of German troops waited anxiously. One Panzer commander hailed another officer from his tank turret: "Good-bye, Lieutenant, see you in America!"[24] At exactly 5:30 A.M., German artillery exploded, signaling the beginning of the German counteroffensive few Allied leaders expected. Along an 85-mile-long (137-kilometer-long) front, mortars, rockets, and artillery opened fire, shaking the ground and dislodging snow from the trees of the Ardennes forest. Tanks revved up and moved forward by the hundreds. German flatcars mounted with heavy siege guns blasted 14-inch (36-centimeter) shells to their targets situated miles away in the fog-shrouded distance. The Ardennes Offensive was under way. As German units moved anxiously forward, they not only had the immediate advantage of surprise, but of superior numbers. The Wehrmacht troops outnumbered the Allies in the region three-to-one. In the specific, designated areas of assault concentration, they enjoyed a combat ratio of ten-to-one.

Across the frozen, snow-covered ground, German infantrymen advanced, wearing white winter uniforms. They moved in formidable units by the dozen, advancing slowly, their weapons poised for action. Behind them huge German searchlights, a new design, lit up the night sky, casting a white flash of dazzlingly bright light and illuminating the startled American GIs encamped in frontline positions. There was a German presence everywhere, advancing through the trees, tanks rumbling, crashing across open ground. Historian John Toland described the scene of terror spreading across the previously inky blackness of a winter's night:

> In the north, infantrymen of Sepp Dietrich's 6th panzer army burst into the [U.S.] 99th division's forward positions. As they did, planes of a new design came out of the east with a strange crackling roar, streaking by at unbelievable speed. The Germans looked up, suddenly realizing these were the new jets. They cheered, wild with excitement. Hitler's "miraculous weapons" were a fact. Even the hard-bitten veterans who had been pummeled in Russia and chased across France felt new hope. Exultantly they swept forward, leaping and screaming and waving their rifles.[25]

The 6th Panzer army struck hard against two American units early that morning, the 2nd and 99th divisions of the 5th corps. Although the 2nd division, which had seen a lot of action throughout the war, responded to the discovery of the German advance quickly and took to their guns, the men of the 99th division, who had faced little previous combat, were slower to respond with force. The troops of the 99th had been shivering in their snow-rimmed foxholes for weeks prior to the offensive, having already lost more than 800 men in their ranks to "frostbite, pneumonia, and trench foot."[26] According to Ambrose, the 99th gave the Germans a hard fight but most of their weapons, like those of the majority of their comrades up and down the line of German advance, were only small arms—rifles, pistols, and bazookas. The men of 5th corps managed to hold the Germans off of Eisenborn Ridge, despite heavy fire from the enemy. The 99th infantry division, wrote author Thomas E. Greiss, "put up so fierce a defense that the Germans were forced to commit tanks which had been designated for the exploitation."[27] Dietrich's tanks still managed to break through at the Losheim Gap, a portion of the Ardennes barely held by the U.S. 14th armored division. The 6th SS Panzer army had been driven south, however, not west as planned, by hard American fighting and resistance.

As Dietrich moved forward, he turned his tanks toward the U.S. 106th division and thus engaged another American unit with little combat experience. The 106th had only been in the Ardennes for less than a week, so combat was new to many of its troops. The Germans were able to penetrate the lines of the 106th in several places, yet they were unable to make a complete breakthrough, the type that had been anticipated in the offensive's planning. The 6th Panzer ended the day off course, having made less progress than Hitler had expected.

As German infantry moved forward on the first day of fighting, German Panzers waited behind them, anxious to make headway and reach the Meuse in the shortest amount of time. One of the most anxious tank commanders was

Lieutenant Colonel Jochen Peiper, who had been assigned the leadership of the 1st SS Panzer division, part of General Dietrich's 6th Panzer army. Peiper was a seasoned veteran of earlier campaigns, including those on Russian soil. As historian Danny S. Parker said: "Handsome, well educated and a devout Nazi, Peiper had developed a reputation for ruthless and daring armored attack."[28]

Decorated for bravery at the age of 29 with the Knight's Cross of the Iron Cross, the young Peiper was known for his ruthless advances against his enemies. He rarely took prisoners (one earlier campaign had ended with his Panzer forces killing 2,500 of the enemy and capturing only three), and he lived for battle. He thought little of any superior officer who had not been through the fire of heavy combat, and he was like Hitler, expecting nearly fanatical devotion from the men under his command. As a result, the casualty rate among those who moved under Peiper's orders was often high. Peiper was, in fact, surprised he was still alive at the end of 1944; most of his earlier contemporaries had already been killed in the war.

Before the offensive opened, Peiper was informed that he was to have a key role in the advance through the Ardennes. Hitler had high hopes for the 6th Panzer army and anticipated Dietrich's units would "fight fanatically."[29] Peiper's superior did not inform Peiper about the offensive until two days before December 16. The Panzer commander was expected to make real progress that first day and advance his tanks nearly 50 miles (81 kilometers) within the offensive's first 24 hours, which would place the 1st SS Panzer division on the banks of the Meuse. His commander told the young SS officer what he expected: "Drive fast and hold the reins loose."[30] Peiper passed the word on to his tank commanders, ordering them to avoid any distractions. "He forbade firing into small groups of the enemy. He forbade looting.

General Dwight Eisenhower, supreme commander of the Allied forces, is seen here with U.S. Generals Bradley, Gerow, and Collins. Eisenhower mustered his troops after determining that the German buildup was a separate offensive rather than simply a counterattack.

Just keep moving,"[31] described Ambrose. Official word of the German advance into the Ardennes on December 16 did not reach the supreme Allied commander, Dwight Eisenhower, until that evening. At his headquarters in Versailles just outside Paris, General Eisenhower, having just been promoted to the rank of five-star general, was briefed on the German attack that had opened that morning. General Omar Bradley had recently arrived by car from his field headquarters in Luxembourg. The two American generals absorbed the news. Bradley was unconvinced the German attack was anything of any real importance. An hour later, however, a second communiqué arrived: The morning attack had included a minimum of 12 German divisions. Eisenhower began to move, understanding he was looking at "a counter-offensive, not a counterattack."[32] He gave Bradley orders to deliver the 7th armored division to the town of St. Vith and the 12th armored to the southern end of the assault at Echternach.

The 7th armored division was in the field far to the north of Monschau, the northern end of the line for the German counteroffensive. When the divisional command received orders to move out, the troops immediately began "loading their trucks, fueling their Shermans and half-tracks, studying road maps of the Ardennes. They were expected in St. Vith in seven hours."[33] St. Vith was one of a handful of towns in the Ardennes that were seen as crucial to both the Germans and the Americans. As Parker observed: "The side which controlled key road junctions would have a distinct advantage. The critical communication centers were Bastogne, on the main Arlon-Liege highway; St. Vith, another important road junction; and Marche, on both the Sedan-Liege and Brussels-Luxembourg highways."[34]

Eisenhower's quick response to the situation he was facing showed determination, insight, and sober judgment. Adolf Hitler had planned the Ardennes Offensive, assuming his forces would advance for two or three days before the Allied commander even understood what he was up against. The German leader also assumed, incorrectly, that Eisenhower would have to talk with Roosevelt and Churchill before making a decision, which meant more days would pass before he could mobilize against the advancing Germans. That was, after all, how Hitler typically hamstrung his Wehrmacht commanders. Eisenhower wasted no time, however. With decisive action, he moved to match Hitler's forces in the Ardennes, looking to hit hard against Hitler's left and right flanks. As historian Stephen

Ambrose described the supreme Allied commander's judgment and decisions:

> What he had done was textbook stuff from World War I —the place to hold a penetration is at the shoulders. It is more important to limit the width of the salient than its depth. But if it took no special genius to figure out what to do, it did take a leap into the mind of the enemy commander. Eisenhower made that leap on the night of December 16. He saw what no one else around him saw, that not only was this a major offensive, but that it was the best thing that could happen.[35]

In Eisenhower's mind, the Germans had now moved out of their fortified positions on their own borders, had abandoned the relative security of their Siegfried Line, and had put themselves in harm's way. His military view was that, now, with the Germans advancing, they were "out in the open where American artillery, American tanks, American infantry, American fighter-bombers would be capable of destroying them."[36]

By the end of the first day of the German blitz into the Ardennes, Hitler's timetable for advancement was already behind schedule. The U.S. 99th and 2nd divisions, with help from the U.S. 1st, had turned Dietrich south. On the southern end of the German offensive, the 5th Panzer and 7th army had faced rock-solid resistance from the American 4th infantry division. In the center advance of the offensive, the U.S. 7th armored division and portions of the 106th and the 9th armored division held fast to their positions near St. Vith, just a few miles west of the Our River. German units had broken across portions of the American line of defense, but they had failed in one of their important goals for the day— taking control of crossroad intersections "that would allow their tanks to roam free behind the American lines."[37]

For the moment, however, any gains that had been made on the first day were thrilling to the German troops pushing through the Ardennes; they were on the offensive. One German Panzer radioman summed up the initial sense of euphoria felt by those Wehrmacht troops who were involved: "We had begun to act like a beaten army. Now, moving forward, the men were extremely happy and filled with enthusiasm. Everywhere there were signs of renewed hope. I never thought the attack would change the tide of the war. But it was a moment to enjoy."[38]

Not all Germans fighting that first day of the Watch on the Rhine were happy with the results, though. General Field Marshal Rundstedt, while admitting that the offensive had completely surprised the Americans, felt the advance had not made adequate progress. He noted "stubborn resistance in major enemy strongpoints three to five kilometers [three miles] behind the frontlines."[39] He also noted that "as a result of the bad weather and bridging conditions, the anticipated rapid advance of the panzer formations had not yet taken place."[40] In response, Hitler ordered the 3rd Panzer grenadier division, waiting in reserve east of Monschau, into the fight to bolster General Dietrich's limited advance. Despite such negative reports, the führer was elated by the day's progress. From his headquarters in the Eagle's Nest outside Frankfurt, an excited Hitler telephoned one of his field generals, Hermann Balck, whose forces were holding the German left flank south of the Ardennes, and gave him the news of the day's success. "Balck! Balck!" the German leader shouted into the telephone. "Everything has changed in the West! Success—complete success—is now in our grasp!"[41]

As for Peiper, he reached the Lanzerath area, just west of Losheim, by midnight of the first day of the offensive. He had been ordered there during the fighting once the

advance of the German 3rd parachute division had been
halted. He had beaten a path to Lanzerath despite running
into minefields, where explosions had destroyed six of his
tanks and half-track personnel carriers. Ironically, the mines
had been planted by the Germans months earlier to stop an
Allied advance. Although he had been expected to advance
on December 16 a distance of 50 miles (81 kilometers), his
initial early forward movement amounted only to approximately 15 miles (24 kilometers).

That night, infantry commanders informed Peiper
they had faced a full day of stiff resistance from American
infantry units, but Peiper was in no mood to keep still.
While his tanks had been sent into the offensive behind
infantry forces, he did not intend to remain at the mercy
of their slow advance. At midnight, he gave orders to
his men to prepare to move their Panzers forward at
4:00 A.M. on December 17. As he pulled out, dashing west
at the following dawn, Peiper's armored column was
impressive. According to Ambrose, "He put two Panther
tanks in front of the column, followed by a series of
armored half-tracks and then another half dozen tanks,
with 30 captured American trucks behind them, and
16 88s at the rear. . . . Peiper was now loose behind
American lines."[42]

After three hours of pushing forward, Peiper stopped
his column, a spearhead far ahead of nearly any other
German force, and filled his vehicles with captured American
gasoline. He continued his straight western route toward
the town of Malmedy. Running nearly linearly along the
Elsenborn Ridge, the high ground in that region of the
Ardennes, he forced back units of the American 99th and
2nd divisions. Two whole regiments of the 106th laid down
their arms, allowing the Germans to capture 7,500 men, the
largest single capture of the enemy during the entire war.
Peiper's spearhead actions had broken a serious hole in the

Nazi armored divisions containing Panther tanks, such as these, nearly over-whelmed Allied forces during the opening hours of the Ardennes Offensive.

American defenses. It would prove to be one of many on December 17. After more than 24 hours of fighting, the thinly scattered American units, most of which had fought valiantly, were starting to feel the overwhelming rush of sheer German numbers.

By dawn on December 17, the first units of the U.S. 7th armored division reached their destination at Bastogne. General Bruce Clarke, commander of combat command B, arrived in an old Mercedes-Benz, loaned to him by a fellow general. Only then did Major General Troy Middleton, commander of the 8th corps, inform Clarke that his men had been reassigned to St. Vith, about 30 miles (48 kilometers) to the northwest. There, as Middleton said in Toland's book, "General Jones [is] in some trouble out on the Schnee Eifel. Two regiments of the 106th are marooned there."[43]

The bulk of the 7th armored was already on its way

toward St. Vith. They were approaching the town from the east, advancing along the main road between Vielsalm and St. Vith. Their progress was slowed by the American military traffic headed west, as forward Ardennes units surrendered their field positions to the advancing Germans. Like fish swimming up a stiff current, the U.S. 7th was only able to advance a few miles an hour. As one U.S. major observed on the afternoon of December 17: "It was already 1515 [3:15 P.M.] and from the looks of the road jam, neither the tanks nor anything else was going to reach St. Vith for a long time,"[44] as quoted in Eisenhower's account. General Clarke arrived that afternoon from Bastogne and found the slow progress of his tanks unacceptable, especially since his forces had left the road to make way for the retreating units and their trucks.

"What's happened here?" he demanded of his operations officer, who was on the scene.

The response: "General, this lieutenant colonel told me he was going to use the road anyway and he'd shoot me if I got in his way."

In no time, Clarke had tracked down the problematic lieutenant colonel and was making his orders clear: "You get your trucks off this road so my tanks can get up here. If there's any shooting done around this place, I'll start it."[45] The road stayed open, and within 30 minutes, the advance units of Clarke's 7th armored showed up. Clarke told them what to do: "Keep going down this road. You'll run into a great big lieutenant colonel. His name is Riggs. Tell him you're attached to him and he'll tell you what to do."[46]

Clarke soon faced other problems, though: The artillery attached to the 7th armored division had been blocked off by Peiper's advance. For the moment, the 275th armored field artillery battalion would have to provide the 7th's only artillery support. By nightfall, some elements of the

7th armored had reached St. Vith and began taking up positions in a horseshoe perimeter on high ground east of the town. By 8:00 P.M., General Clarke's command, including infantry, cavalry, and tank units, had reached the small Belgian town, and throughout the night, Clarke put his men into position. By 4:00 A.M. on December 18, the third day of the German offensive opened with the American defense of St. Vith in "fairly decent shape."[47] Clarke offered direct field command of the 7th's positions to General Jones, but he declined, insisting "this was completely a 7th armored division fight."[48]

The Massacre at Malmedy

During the second day of the offensive, on December 17, in the midst of heavy and destructive fighting up and down the German offensive line, one act of violence drew more condemnation than any other—an incident outside the little town of Malmedy.

On December 17, the U.S. 7th armored division moved from Heerlen, Holland, bound for the town of St. Vith in the Ardennes to help relieve the U.S. 106th division, which had been encircled by the Germans. One of the 7th's units, battery B of the 285th field artillery observation battalion, consisting of about 140 men, was on its way along a road leading to Malmedy. Suddenly, near the small town of Baugnez, German tanks crossed the road in front of the truck convoy of American soldiers. They were part of Peiper's 1st SS Panzer division. The Germans fired on the trucks and the Americans surrendered.

The captive GIs were then taken to a field near the Café Bodarwe at a road intersection. As SS soldiers guarded the American captives, they began taking items from their prisoners, including watches, rings, even clothing. When a U.S. army captain protested, shouting, "You're violating the Geneva Convention," an SS trooper pulled out his P-38 sidearm and shot him in the head.[*]

This shocking execution of one prisoner soon escalated as a German tank gunner, later identified as SS Sturmann Georg Fleps, fired his handgun into the group of American captives. Others joined in and shots were fired on

That evening, Wehrmacht General Hasso von Manteuffel, who had spent the day pushing his men slowly across the Schnee Eifel toward St. Vith, met with his superior General Field Marshall Walther Model. Model was concerned that Manteuffel had not progressed adequately toward the vital crossroads at St. Vith.

"We'll take it tomorrow," Manteuffel assured Model.

"I expect you to," stated Model. The field marshal then assigned an additional brigade to Manteuffel to assure the successful capture of St. Vith. Manteuffel understood the urgency of his mission.

top of one another. One SS trooper was later quoted as shouting, "Kill them all!" ** Machine guns mounted on a pair of tanks unloaded on the trapped Americans and the majority of them fell instantly, dead where they had stood. The last man standing was dropped by two pistol shots from Fleps.

Some of the victims lay still alive among the dead and moaned or screamed in pain. The SS men then began to move about the field, killing the survivors. Some were able to make a break into the nearby woods. In all, 17 Americans survived the killing spree later called the "Malmedy Massacre." Dozens of their comrades had been executed that day in a snow-covered field. Said one survivor: "We didn't have a chance." ***

As the story of the massacre spread up and down American lines, many U.S. soldiers decided to refuse to accept the surrender of any SS trooper. The U.S. 26th division even issued an order to its field troops: "No SS troops or paratroopers will be taken prisoner, but will be shot on sight." The order was later nullified, but it is certain that, because of the Malmedy Incident, some German troops who later attempted surrender were dispatched with a vengeful form of battlefield justice.

*   *Source:* Quoted in Danny S. Parker, *Battle of the Bulge: Hitler's Ardennes Offensive, 1944–1945.* Conshohocken, PA: Combined Publishing, 1991, p. 122.

**   *Source:* Ibid.

*** *Source:* Ibid., p. 123.

"We've got to take St. Vith tomorrow," he repeated to his superior. "And the brigade may swing the balance."[49]

Eisenhower was busy on December 17 studying his maps of the Ardennes and delivering orders for reinforcements to be dispatched to the new front. Stationed in Reims, the 101st and 82nd airborne, which had participated in Montgomery's "Market-Garden" Offensive just three months earlier, were ordered by General Eisenhower to key locations in the Ardennes. The 82nd was delivered to match the German right flank, focusing on Elsenborn, located behind the Elsenborn Ridge and northwest of the Losheim Gap. The supreme commander sent the 101st airborne into the city of Bastogne on the southern flank of Hitler's advancing forces. Eisenhower considered Bastogne, a significant crossroads, a "must" to defend and therefore augmented the 101st by ordering the 10th armored division, part of Patton's 3rd army, to the same destination. Within hours, thousands of paratroopers and other infantrymen needed transportation to the field of battle. Eisenhower ordered the truck drivers of the Red Ball Express to abandon all other orders and turn themselves into troop transport vehicles. On December 17, only the second day of fighting, 60,000 American combatants were delivered into the Ardennes theater by more than 10,000 trucks, along with tons of supplies, ammunition, and much-needed fuel.

Although the German troops sent into the Ardennes vastly outnumbered the Americans they initially encountered, the U.S. forces in the region had more artillery at their disposal than the Germans, as well as more aircraft. The ability of the Americans to transport almost anything—supplies, troops, ammunition, the wounded—was much greater than that of the Germans, thanks to the wonderful durability of their jeeps and the ox-like stamina of their two-and-a-half-ton trucks, the Ford

A huge supply and transportation operation called "The Red Ball Express" delivered military supplies to the Allied forces in France in 1944. Materiel was taken by railroad car to the end of the rail lines and then transferred to trucks.

model known popularly among the field soldiers as "deuce-and-a-half."

While the Ardennes continued to swirl with activity as German and American forces jockeyed for positions, the German Luftwaffe took heavily to the air on December 17. With a cloud cover at 5,000 feet (1,524 meters), German planes engaged in between 600 and 700 missions, or sorties, providing air support for Wehrmacht ground troops. The skies over the Ardennes also witnessed 1,000 American flights as the two air forces fought one another for supremacy. Much of the action in the skies was centered over the town of St. Vith. American planes armed with 500-pound (227-kilogram) bombs dropped their ordnance loads on German positions.

In Ambrose's recollection, one U.S. pilot described the action he both witnessed and carried out:

> I saw a [German] Thunderbolt and a [Focke-Wulf] going down in flames. . . . Enemy aircraft all over the place. . . . Our controller . . . was calm and calling in a prime target—a pontoon bridge across the River Roer. . . . We used our bombs and rockets on the vehicles and the bridge then set up several strafing passes. There were burning vehicles and some damage to the bridge when we left after about 20 minutes.[50]

Here and there along their self-appointed front, the Germans pushed forward on December 17. There were serious problems impeding their overall progress, such as the narrow, winding road system that was hardly adequate to handle the number of Wehrmacht vehicles, many being heavy tanks. There was a shortage of available trucks to transport infantry. While new German jets zoomed overhead, it was ironic that the majority of the German artillery guns were carried to the field by horses. Troops pushed hurriedly toward one Ardennes village, captured it, then had to hold their positions before advancing to the next town, when the roads ahead of them were passable again. With Christmas just around the corner, some Wehrmacht actually stopped in village shops to buy presents.

Although there was a major breakthrough in the center of the offensive line, in a straight line toward the key crossroads of Bastogne, the advances made by Peiper to the north were probably more important. Only the roads between his field position and the Meuse River could hold him back from advancing straight to Antwerp, Hitler's ultimate goal. By noon, his tanks blasted an American truck convoy to pieces and moved on. Peiper was intent on stopping for no

Nazi SS Lieutenant Colonel Peiper, Panzer commander, played a major role in the fighting in the Ardennes. He was known as a ruthless, aggressive fighter and was in charge of the German soldiers who fired on U.S. prisoners of war near Malmedy, France.

reason; any targets he chose to engage had to be worth his time. By 4:00 P.M., the village of Stavelot on the Ambleve River loomed into view. In the town, Peiper saw another American truck convoy. Unleashing his Panzers on the

Americans, as well as his infantry, the Americans pulled
back and abandoned Stavelot. By nightfall, no one had
pushed farther on the second day of the German counteroffensive than General Peiper. He, however, was not happy;
he knew it had taken him 36 hours to reach Stavelot. In
1940, when Hitler unleashed his blitzkrieg through the
same region, a Wehrmacht armored column had reached
Stavelot in less than 10 hours.

December 17 also saw the advance of the 18th *volks-
grenadiers*, who captured bridges at Schonberg on the road
to St. Vith, and Andler on the Our River. Another German
regiment to the south fought near the town of Bleialf and
then surrounded American forces in the Schnee Eifel. By
noon, a German battalion captured towns just five miles
(eight kilometers) east of St. Vith. Then, by nightfall,
Wehrmacht advance units were just two miles (three
kilometers) out of St. Vith. While this advance signaled
menacingly for the Americans in the region, there were
U.S. successes that same day in that same region, wrote
Parker: "Artillery concentrations on Schonberg, an
American air attack in the afternoon and the stand made
by elements of the 14th armored cavalry at Heum took
much of the bite out of the German push."[51] The U.S.
5th armored division was sent to Monschau to help hold
American positions there. The 99th infantry battalion
was ordered to Malmedy. Three U.S. battalions were
sent to Spa, where General Courtney Hodges and his
1st army headquarters were situated in the Hotel Britannica
and faced a host of German parachutists just outside
the city. Enemy patrols had also been reported in the
immediate area.

As Hodges studied his situation, he determined that his
main opponent was General "Sepp" Dietrich's 6th Panzers.
He realized Dietrich could sweep past him and reach
the Meuse by continuing straight west, or the German

commander could feint and slip hard to the north, which would allow him not only to bypass altogether the 1st army, but any and all Allied armies scattered across Holland. Hodges knew he must halt Dietrich in his tracks. His immediate dilemma was simple: Where should he make his stand in the face of quickly advancing Wehrmacht forces? After studying his maps, he noticed the strategic position of a pair of hills that formed Elsenborn Ridge, running parallel and just north of the main road leading to the Meuse River. This high ground could serve as a reasonable defensive position. Before noon, General Hodges telephoned Eisenhower at supreme headquarters, American expeditionary forces (SHAEF) outside Paris. It was this phone call that prompted Eisenhower to dispatch the 82nd airborne division to Elsenborn Ridge.

The second day of the Watch on the Rhine counter-offensive ended with several American positions having been routed and thousands of U.S. soldiers on the run toward the west, abandoning their equipment, burning fuel dumps, and fleeing for their lives. These retreats were often chaotic and spontaneous, as soldier after soldier abandoned his position against odds he considered over-whelming. Just after noon on December 17, as the U.S. 7th armored division reached the Ardennes, the American tanks were met with a horrific sight described by Major Donald Boyer in Ambrose's book: "a constant stream of traffic hurtling to the rear and nothing going to the front. We realized that this was not a convoy moving to the rear; it was a case of 'every dog for himself.' It wasn't orderly, it wasn't military, it wasn't a pretty sight. We were seeing American soldiers running away."[52]

"What's a
Texas Leaguer?"

German SS troops captured and burned American trucks on their push into Allied lines on the Western front. Destruction of such vehicles and bridges was a vital stratagem during the Battle of the Bulge.

On the following day, December 18, the number of retreating U.S. forces was even greater. Yet even as American forces turned tail in the Ardennes, moving down roads out of harm's way, they were met with reinforcements, men dispatched to the field of fire to stand against the German Wehrmacht advance. Among them were the men of the 101st airborne, headed for the town of Bastogne.

Just after sunrise on December 18, the morning of the third day of the offensive, General Peiper entered the town of Stavelot, only to find the village abandoned and the Americans gone. The retreating GIs had not left town before they set their fuel dump on fire, though, leaving Peiper with no free fuel; he pushed forward anyway. That he did not stop long enough to secure the town and leave it defended would be a decision he would later regret. Running along the right flank of Dietrich's army, Peiper's 1st SS Panzer division fought across the Ambleve River at Stavelot, smashing all resistance, including a defense attempt by the U.S. 526th infantry battalion whose men had barricaded themselves for a fight at the bridge. Moving as always like a man driven toward a solitary goal, Peiper pushed on to the next bridge, located at Trois Ponts, just three to four miles to the southwest. When he reached the town, his lead tank suddenly exploded as hidden charges were detonated by the U.S. 51st engineer combat battalion. The unfortunate tank and its crew plunged down into the icy waters of the Salm River.

Peiper was angry, since the destroyed bridge cut off his intended route west. When reflecting after the war on the impact of the destruction of the span, he stated: "If only we had taken the bridge at Trois Ponts intact and had enough fuel, it would have been a simple matter to drive through to the Meuse River early that day."[53] Thwarted, he backed up and turned to the northwest along the Ambleve river valley, capturing the town of La Gleize. At Cheneux, Peiper's tanks crossed the bridge over the River Ambleve, then headed toward Werbomont. Here, a group of American fighter-bombers flew and strafed Peiper's column around 1:30 P.M. The U.S. planes knocked out three of Peiper's tanks and five half-tracks. The wrecked vehicles then had to be pushed off and clear of the road before Peiper could advance, a loss of two hours' time he could never make up. This delay allowed the men of the U.S. 291st engineer combat battalion, who had heard the distant strafing attack and understood that the Germans were approaching, enough time to prepare a welcome for Peiper's Panzers. As the tanks approached the Neufmoulin Bridge near Lienne Creek, the engineers set off dynamite charges on the bridge just as it came into the Nazi tank commander's view. All Peiper could do was swear: "The damned engineers!"[54]

Again, Peiper had no choice but to retrace his tread tracks back to La Gleize in search of a new route to yet another bridge. He was now facing another problem altogether, though, one he could not solve immediately: His war machines were running out of fuel. The legendary Wehrmacht Panzer commander had reason for concern. Behind him came the 501st heavy Panzer battalion with its Tiger tanks, which reached the River Ambleve at Stavelot then La Gleize in support of Peiper's spearhead movements. The U.S. 30th infantry division, however, under the command of Major General Leland S. Hobbs, reached Stavelot in the afternoon, as well as Malmedy to the northeast. Hobbs's position put him behind Peiper's army and in the way of the German general's rear supply lines.

Meanwhile, ten miles (16 kilometers) southwest of Stavelot, SS Panzer grenadiers reached the village of Recht, just five miles (eight kilometers) northwest of the vital crossroads of St. Vith. Here, they engaged units of the U.S. 7th armored division which had just recently reached the region. The fighting pushed the Americans three miles (five kilometers) south to the town of Poteau. On the morning of December 18, German units fought to push the U.S. forces out of Poteau. The town was so close to St. Vith that orders were issued from the 7th armored division for the town to be liberated at once. After a hard-fought battle that afternoon, the SS Panzer grenadiers retreated back to Recht.

At that moment, just six miles (ten kilometers) away, the German 46th army corps was outside St. Vith, preparing to launch an attack against American positions in the town. In three assaults, the Germans were repulsed, taking heavy casualties. The field of action in this center portion of the Wehrmacht advance was widespread. While fighting unfolded at St. Vith, the German 62nd grenadier division was engaging the 424th regiment of the 106th division at Winterspelt, just southeast of St. Vith. The fighting there was heavy, as the town was exchanged back and forth several times. Back at St. Vith, the Americans held their positions with greater resistance to the increasing number of German units fighting against them.

Elsewhere, at Bastogne, Wehrmacht General Manteuffel sent his two Panzer divisions to destroy American road-blocks outside the town. By midnight on December 18, the blocks had been removed and the 2nd Panzer division stood six miles (ten kilometers) north of Bastogne at the village crossroads of Noville. Additional German units were only three miles (five kilometers) out of Bastogne, arriving from the east, having passed the town of Eschweiler ten miles (16 kilometers) out at 3:00 P.M. To the northeast, the 11th Panzer division passed through Heinerscheid and Troisverges, northeast of Bastogne. The Americans at Bastogne were not fully aware of their situation, but German forces were moving in to surround the town. Additional German divisions and armies were advancing on other otherwise sleepy towns in the Ardennes by the evening of December 18.

Yet even as the day had brought German advances, the high command of the Wehrmacht was not pleased with the field progress of its forces. Although it was noted that Peiper's combat group had pushed ahead and broken out behind American lines, General Rundstedt wrote in his evening report that "no real progress by the panzer formations" had taken place.[55] He did order forces to continue pushing through the night without significant

Lieutenant General Manteuffel with Colonels Lorenz and Langkeit. On December 18, the high command of the Wehrmacht told Hitler that the counterattack was not advancing as planned. Hitler kept his original goal of reaching Antwerp, Belgium.

breaks, but he still believed the overall counteroffensive that Hitler had imagined was doomed to failure. Rundstedt wrote:

> We should abandon the offensive and prepare to defend the area we have gained. Sepp Dietrich's forces are held up between Monschau and Malmedy. St. Vith had not been taken. We have only just reached Bastogne, which ought to have been taken on D plus 1 [December 17]. We have not made the most of our initial surprise. The offensive has never gathered speed due to the icy roads and the pockets of resistance which have forced us to lay in full scale attacks.[56]

There were other doubters among the German commanders. General Model stated in his report, "the third day of the attack is marked by the successful breakthrough on the broad front between Stavelot and Bastogne."[57] He did not believe in the overall possibilities of turning the tide of war by continuing the counteroffensive. This had been the führer's plan from the beginning. It was Model's opinion on the night of December 18 that the "Big Solution had failed."[58] When the pessimistic opinions of Rundstedt and Model reached Hitler that evening, he castigated them. Even the German leader was concerned enough about the situation, however, that he ordered multiple units he had reserved for an attack north of the Ardennes into the region of the main offensive to bolster flagging German forces. Still, Hitler retained his original goal of the Watch on the Rhine: advancing his forces to Antwerp.

Although the offensive was only three days old, by the morning of December 19, the German field armies were facing a serious fuel shortage. American air bombing was partially responsible for the fuel shortage at the front, as well as a shortage of other supplies bound for the fighting armies of the Third Reich in the Ardennes. On December 18, 800 medium Allied bombers, escorted by an equal number of fighter planes, had dropped their ordnance on supply depots and other crucial German targets behind the advance lines of the offensive. Even without this crucial bombing, the amount of fuel Hitler had promised before the offensive had opened had not been properly routed or delivered. The need was so desperate that reserve fuel was rerouted from other fronts. Even as plans and promises were made by December 18 to deliver 4,500 tons (4,572 metric tons) of gasoline and oil to the front, truck transport was in short supply. Just getting the gas where it was needed had been problematic since the first day of planning the Ardennes Offensive.

For those mechanized forces that the Germans were able to move, even slowly, on December 18, the weather ushered in icy rain, which caused many of the unpaved roads in the Ardennes to become thick with mud.

General Eisenhower met with his senior commanders on the morning of December 19 in a barracks building near the World War I battlefield of Verdun, France. There was little hope on the faces of those gathered to discuss the previous few days of fighting and their plans for tomorrow. Eisenhower, however, did not intend to give the Germans any points for their advances since December 16, stating, "The present situation is to be regarded as one of opportunity for us and not of disaster."[59] He insisted that his generals be as upbeat as possible, and they did not disappoint him. The majority of those present were ready to turn the three-day-old German counteroffensive around with an Allied offensive of their own. There was general agreement: If American and British forces could limit the width of the "bulge" penetration the Germans had accomplished already and contain it between the towns of Bastogne on the south flank and St. Vith on the north, the offensive could only advance so far before supplies would be a problem for the Wehrmacht. The Allies could easily cut off supply lines behind the restricted German advance.

One concern at the meeting, among many, was whether the town of Bastogne was still held by American forces. There was some anxiety that the key Ardennes village might become surrounded by the enemy. Whether or not Bastogne became encircled or when, Eisenhower asked General Patton how quickly he could get his 3rd army, tanks and all, situated south of the German salient, to Bastogne.

"When can you start?" the supreme commander asked the feisty tank commander.

"As soon as you're through with me," Patton responded, without hesitation.[60]

General Patton (right), commander of the 3rd U.S. army, is seen here with supreme Allied commander Eisenhower. The two career military men had a long history of working together.

Asked to clarify his response, Patton assured Eisenhower and his fellow generals that his men, three full divisions, would be in position to attack German forces at Bastogne in 48 hours. Eisenhower found the dramatic claim unrealistic. December 21 would be too soon for Patton to have three complete divisions battle-ready and in position. He instructed his gung-ho comrade to take an extra day or two and make certain he and his men were ready and in full strength.

Patton was eager for the fight that he knew would be one of the greatest of his military career. He told General Bradley that day: "Brad, this time the Kraut's stuck his head in the meatgrinder, and this time I've got hold of the handle."[61] Eisenhower did not realize how prepared Patton actually was that morning to bring his men into a fight at Bastogne in just two days. He had already ordered his staff to prepare "three concepts of how the 3rd U.S. army might be employed. Each concept had been assigned a code word, which he had left with his chief of staff . . . so by merely uttering a single word over the telephone, Patton could launch his army according to anticipated orders."[62]

Before the meeting ended, Eisenhower gave explicit instructions to Patton to launch his offensive at Bastogne on December 22 or December 23. He guaranteed the commander of the 3rd army that he would provide air support. Eisenhower also announced he would order offensive action on the northern flank of the German line once the situation at Bastogne was secure. The meeting completed, Patton left the conference room, telephoned his staff, and gave them the appropriate code word. Each of his army's units—the 4th armored, the 80th infantry division, and the 26th infantry division—knew what it was to do.

Eisenhower walked Patton to the door, and the two generals joked with one another. The supreme commander had just been promoted to a five-star general on the day the Ardennes Offensive opened.

"Funny thing, George," said Eisenhower. "Every time I get another star I get attacked."

"And every time you get attacked, Ike," ribbed Patton, "I have to bail you out."[63]

In all, General Patton was to move six divisions in short order, including his 3rd and 12th corps, from their positions at the Saar front, along a line stretching from

Bastogne on their left flank, to Diekirch at their center, to Echternach on their right. (Echternach had been the German left flank at the opening of the offensive on the morning of December 16.) The movement of Patton's 3rd army would become legendary. Within just a few days, more than 133,000 vehicles were rerouted over a combined distance of 1.5 million miles (2.4 million kilometers), most of them covering ground layered with snow, ice, and mud. Behind the advancing mobile forces,

General George S. Patton

E ven the Germans respected Patton. One Wehrmacht general gave him high praise: "His operations impressed us enormously, probably because he came closest to our concept of the classical military commander." General von Manteuffel agreed: "Patton! No doubt about this. He was a brilliant panzer army commander." *

Lieutenant General George S. Patton, Jr., the leader of the U.S. 3rd army, was one of the most complicated and contradictory, yet brilliant, military leaders of the entire war. His style drew the attention of both his superiors and German commanders, as well as the press, who loved to quote the tank commander saying such deathless phrases as, "In war, death is incidental, but loss of time is criminal." **

He came from an old Southern family and had grown up fascinated by all things military. He attended the U.S. Military Academy at West Point, graduating with the class of 1909. As a lieutenant, Patton had accompanied General John J. Pershing in his punitive expedition to capture the Mexican gunman Pancho Villa in 1916, and had served as an aide to Pershing during World War I. In 1917, he commanded the 304th light tank brigade in the battle at St. Mihiel and fought in the 1918 Argonne Offensive, one of the last of the war before the surrender of the Germans. Following the war, he remained in uniform, commanding the U.S. 2nd armored division, then the 1st armored corps, while stationed at Fort Benning, Georgia.

When World War II drew in the United States as a combatant, Patton was dispatched to North Africa in 1942, where his 2nd corps saw success against the forces of General Rommel. His next field of battle was Sicily, then a field

Patton's supply echelons kept pace and shipped 62,000 tons of supplies to his advancing army.

By December 20, General Eisenhower had ordered British tank commander Montgomery to organize an attack from the north against the right flank units of the German offensive. He gave Montgomery command of the U.S. 1st and 9th armies, while giving General Bradley command of the southern flank. (Patton took his orders directly from Bradley.)

command in the Normandy landing. It was Patton's 3rd army that had forced the St. Lo breakout of Allied forces from Normandy into the heart of France.

As a field commander, Patton was brilliant. He believed firmly in moving through the field with speed (an American blitzkrieg), constantly pushing the enemy, and never letting up. He loved tank combat and placed himself as close to the fighting as possible, observing: "I want the men of the third army to know where I am, and that I risk the same danger that they do." *** Often his own personal bravery and self-styled arrogance instilled confidence in his men. In a letter written to his son, Patton observed of himself: "Leadership . . . is the one thing that wins battles. I have it—but I'll be damned if I can define it." ****

He loved military showiness, parades, and other elements of pomp and circumstance. Personally flamboyant, he wore a pair of ivory-handled, .45-caliber Colt revolvers. Patton believed so strongly in his skill and tactics as a tank commander that after his army broke through enemy positions to occupy the town of Bastogne, he wrote that his actions amounted to "the most brilliant operation we have thus far performed, and it is in my opinion the outstanding achievement of this war. This *is my biggest battle*." *****

---

*   Source: Quoted in Danny S. Parker, *Battle of the Bulge: Hitler's Ardennes Offensive, 1944–1945*. Conshohocken, PA: Combined Publishing, 1991, p. 38.

**   *Source:* Ibid.

***   *Source:* Ibid.

*****   *Source:* Ibid.

*****   *Source:* Ibid.

As December 19, a Tuesday, dawned, the Germans faced more problems. Dietrich's army had not progressed well from the first day of the offensive and on the fourth day, his army was again repelled by stiff American fighting. Eisenhower had managed to reinforce the northern forces adequately, and they held despite every attempt made by Dietrich to crack the American veneer. He ordered the 12th SS Panzer division to the south to break the flank position of the U.S. 1st division at Butgenbach, a town situated in the eastern region of the Ardennes, but heavy American artillery on both December 19 and 20, as well as "strong enemy resistance"[64] from the U.S. 1st division, stymied Dietrich's strategy and held up his field advances. A paratroop drop of 800 men and supplies on December 17 had failed to provide adequate support for Dietrich. Only 200 paratroopers reached their units, while the other 600 hid in the forests of the Ardennes, spending all their time avoiding detection by American patrols.

Other units of the 6th Panzer army had similar difficulties. Peiper had pushed so far ahead of the main column that he was completely out of radio contact with Dietrich. In addition, Peiper had become caught in a trap of his own making. He had pushed so deeply forward, as one officer told him, "without concern for your flanks,"[65] that he was nearly hamstrung. In the River Ambleve region, around La Gleize and Stoumont, his fuel was running low, and when he tried to roll past the town of Targnon, he was attacked by the U.S. 30th infantry division. At the same time, other American units were rushing toward Peiper's positions, since he represented the farthest advance of any German field unit. His logistical supply line had already been cut with the American capture of Stavelot.

By late afternoon on December 19, the U.S. 30th division and units of the 3rd armored were concentrating their attacks against Peiper's advance troops outside Stoumont, just west of La Gleize. There, the U.S. 740th tank battalion attacked the Germans near the town's sanatorium. After the 740th took serious hits that destroyed many of its armored vehicles, the fighting devolved into a hand-to-hand struggle in the town's buildings, including the sanatorium, which changed hands several times that night. The fighting continued for the next couple of days.

During the opening hours of the Ardennes Offensive, Hitler's commando, Otto Skorzeny, and his Panzer brigade 150 did not succeed in their immediate mission. Skorzeny's men were assigned to accompany Peiper's 1st SS Panzer division. The thrust of the Skorzeny mission had been to recruit special units that would wear American and British uniforms, bear appropriate Allied weaponry, and travel in captured Allied tanks, jeeps, and other vehicles. The units were then to travel ahead of the advancing German Panzer tank divisions to the Meuse River in Belgium and seize and hold one or more of the bridges at Engis, Amay, and Huy until the advancing Panzers could cross and meet the Allies at full strength. Beyond this objective, the units were to cause as much confusion for the enemy as possible by cutting communication lines, changing road markers, giving false or inaccurate orders, and in general, damaging Allied morale by spreading false rumors of exceptional German victories in the Ardennes region.

Although the Wehrmacht command had granted Otto Skorzeny limitless authority to requisition, his units went behind Allied lines woefully undersupplied and inadequately trained. His men had received only bits and pieces of captured uniforms of the enemy. On the back of many of the combat jackets was the revealing stamped title POW (prisoner of war), indicating the lack of usable American uniforms at the disposal of the German army. There were not enough steel helmets to go around and American M-1 rifles were in short supply. To mobilize his 3,500 men, Parker noted, Skorzeny had requisitioned "15 Sherman tanks, 32 armored cars, 198 trucks, and 147 jeeps."[66] Most of these vehicles never arrived. By the end of November, just a couple of weeks before the scheduled offensive, Skorzeny's men had been given two M-4 Sherman tanks (which were later abandoned due to transmission problems), six armored cars (only two of them American), six German half-tracks, 57 jeeps, and 74 trucks (only 15 of them were Fords). The remainder of the needed vehicles were German models painted in American green. Concerning some German tanks, altered with pieces of wood painted to resemble the shape of a Sherman tank, Skorzeny later said that they could only trick "very young American recruits—and then only very far away and at night."[67]

Although all Skorzeny's men were supposed to speak English, of the total number of soldiers in the so-called "armored brigade 150," only about 400 of the volunteers had an adequate English vocabulary to dupe any questioning American military police or patrolling scouts. Fewer than a dozen could speak the language with any sense of how to use American slang. The remainder of the cast could say, possibly, "yes" or "no." When Skorzeny discovered how inadequate were the English speaking skills of nearly all his men, he "struck a new low in despondency. I wanted to consign the whole thing to the devil."[68]

To make his disguised troops more believable, Skorzeny established an "American School," in which his volunteer recruits were taught how to use slang and otherwise behave like U.S. GIs. They received instruction in how to chew gum American-style, how to swear effectively, and what gestures to make. They were taught catchphrases as answers to questions they might be asked if they ran up

Patton's 4th armored unit contained Sherman tanks like this one. The Germans had used the element of surprise to win the first few days of the battle, but Eisenhower now depended on Patton to help turn the tide for the Allies.

against American soldiers at checkpoints. If asked by a GI, "Who goes there?" Skorzeny's men were instructed to say something like, "It's okay, Joe, don't mind me." If they were asked to give a password, they were taught to say something to distract the questioner, such as "Aw, go lay an egg!" If pressed for a response, the instructors taught them to swear as a cover, then insist they were in a hurry and running out of patience.[69]

As Skorzeny's men readied to join the Ardennes Offensive on December 16, everyone understood the difficulties of their special mission. To be carried out successfully, the entire scenario hinged on whether the offensive met with slim resistance by the Americans. Skorzeny's operatives, wrote Parker, were to wait until the advancing infantry and Panzer units had moved forward, then race ahead of their comrades to "seize at least two Meuse bridges from among the following possibilities: Amay, Huy, Andenne."[70] The plan called for the commandos to reach the Meuse within the first six hours of the offensive; however, the plan did not exactly work out. Following behind the 1st SS Panzer division, Skorzeny and his forces became part of the German traffic jam that blocked the roads to the west. Although the bulk of Skorzeny's men could not move toward the Meuse, he was still able to dispatch nine jeep teams ahead. Eight of them were able to make it through American security stops, and by nightfall on the first day of the offensive, disguised German jeep teams were moving wherever they chose and causing as much confusion as they could.

These teams met with success as saboteurs, wreaking havoc among the Americans by cutting telephone wires and turning directional signposts, a maneuver that succeeded in directing a 3,000-man American regiment down the wrong road. One jeep team even snapped the cable linking General Omar Bradley, field commander of all American troops, to the U.S. 1st army command in Spa, Belgium. Of the entire Ardennes Offensive force of 250,000 men, only one Skorzeny team, a force of four men, could boast of crossing the Meuse near Amay on December 17. Another team may have been responsible for preventing the Ambleve bridge at Stavelot from being destroyed the following day.

When word spread of these clandestine jeep squads in American uniforms, there was a general panic among the U.S. units in the field. Many knew of Skorzeny's reputation, and the idea of German commandos moving behind enemy lines while passing themselves off as just another group of GIs caused American troops, in the words of General Omar Bradley, "to play cat and mouse with each other each time they met on the road."[71] When

American units approached one another, they would quiz each other, asking for information about popular American culture or facts they thought few Germans would commonly know. The list of questions was endless: Who plays centerfield for the Yankees? What's a Texas Leaguer? Who's married to actress Betty Grable? What's Mickey Mouse's girlfriend's name? The result of such quizzing sometimes caused U.S. military police (MP) to overreact. On December 21, General Bruce Clarke was stopped on the road outside St. Vith. The MP there said he had been told to keep an eye out for a German disguised as a one-star general. Clarke did not prove his identity when he mistakenly identified the Chicago Cubs as an American League team. For 30 minutes, the American general was held in shackles until the errors and misjudgments were sorted out. The following day, General Bradley was stopped at a checkpoint and asked to name the capital of Illinois. When Bradley correctly answered, "Springfield," he was detained by a military policeman who thought Chicago was the state capital.

By the fifth day of the German offensive, several of Skorzeny's men who had driven their jeeps behind American lines had been discovered and captured. Most of them were shot. It was a fear Skorzeny had voiced in the early stages of planning his commando mission. Since his men went into combat wearing the uniforms of their enemy, when captured they were treated as spies, rather than captured soldiers. This allowed American units to try their captives and order their executions in the field rather than treat them as prisoners of war. Three were captured on December 17, just 12 miles (19 kilometers) short of the Meuse, and they were tried days later and shot. Others were taken prisoner, tried, and shot by firing squad, including seven who were captured at Malmedy. A total of 18 of Skorzeny's men faced execution by firing squad.

American soldiers prepare to execute a German spy. Skorzeny's "spy brigade" committed sabotage and sent back useful information about troop movements and bridge traffic, but, when captured, they were not accorded the privileges of the Geneva Convention as prisoners of war.

Despite the general panic created by a handful of jeep teams by December 18, two days after the initiation of the offensive, Skorzeny saw little purpose in attempting to carry out his mission on a full scale. American resistance was unpredictably strong, and the advance of the Panzer divisions so limited that the possibility of success quickly faded. Skorzeny requested permission from Nazi General Peiper, commander of the 6th SS Panzer army, to abandon his mission and allow his men to remove their "Trojan horse disguises" of American uniforms and be utilized as infantry personnel. Peiper and Skorzeny reached an agreement, and the bulk of Skorzeny's men went under Peiper's command.

U.S. infantrymen of the 4th armored division shoot at German troops near Bastogne, Belgium, in December 1944. This kind of ground fire protected the American forces that were under siege inside the town and practically surrounded.

"Nuts!"

In the early morning hours of December 19, German Panzers were preparing to surround Bastogne. Just then, the men of the 101st airborne division began arriving. The arrival at Bastogne of the 101st as well as elements of the 10th armored division would be crucial to the events quickly unfolding around the small, 3,500-person town in the southern Ardennes. These units were able to keep the Germans off the main roads as they moved closer to Bastogne, thus slowing down the progress of the Wehrmacht forces. Beginning on December 19, though, the American forces inside Bastogne were definitely under siege and virtually surrounded. Starting on that date, the Germans began launching repeated attacks against the American positions using

89

15 divisions, including four armored, plus support from heavy artillery fire.

As at several key sites in the Ardennes, December 19 was a critical day of battle preparation for the American forces. Before the day's end, the 101st airborne, the 9th armored, the 705th tank destroyer battalion, and units of the 10th armored had gathered and taken positions for the approaching battle of Bastogne.

For the Americans inside Bastogne, the circumstances were grim. The strategy for the American forces occupying the 20-mile-long (32-kilometer-long) defensive ring outside Bastogne was organized by Lieutenant Colonel Harry Kinnard, operations officer for the 101st. He placed the infantry regiments into "combined arms" teams, each having its own tanks, tank destroyers (TDs), and antitank guns. The teams were assigned a road position to block against a German advance.

Keeping the Germans out of the defensive ring was hardly an easy task. The weather was poor, including subzero temperatures and snowfall. During such weather, the field of battle was covered with heavy ground fog, which covered German advances from view. As one American officer described the situation in Ambrose's book: "Opaque figures in snow suits emerging from nowhere."[72] Much of the fighting was scattered, almost amounting to nothing more than a multitude of deadly skirmishes popping up at various points around the Bastogne ring.

An example of the kind of fighting that took place repeatedly during the siege at Bastogne involved an American squad led by Corporal Robert Bowen, of the 401st glider infantry, 101st airborne. A German unit sneaked past a northwestern perimeter roadblock under cover of darkness and fog, and established its own roadblock between the 101st and Bastogne. Two American squads were dispatched, both under Corporal Bowen. He and his men discussed their options, only to have a tank arrive on their road. The sergeant in command of the tank offered his help, and Bowen, happy for the support, divided his men, sending half on either side of the road approaching the offensive German roadblock. The resulting fight included the squad laying down a blanket of heavy fire, while the tank commander blasted away with his .50-caliber machine guns. Twelve white-clad German soldiers lay dead, and Bowen and his men returned to their home base foxholes.

The following morning, after a freezing night, Bowen's men spotted advancing German infantry. They opened fire at the enemy, and the Germans returned fire with the 11 Panzers accompanying the infantry unit. Bowen's antitank gun stood immobile, its wheel frozen tight. As the German Panzers approached, a second tank destroyer moved in to support Bowen's men just in time to protect them from the heavy tank guns. As a fight developed, a U.S. mortar unit launched 81-mm (three-inch) mortar shells at the advancing Germans. A half-track delivered another squad of troops to augment Bowen's forces and casualties mounted on both sides, wrote Ambrose, "one babbling incoherently and the other screaming. German dead [lay] sprawled in contorted positions."[73] From the rear of the half-track, Bowen grabbed a bazooka and three rounds, then positioned himself to take aim at a German Tiger tank at 200 yards (183 meters). His first round struck the tank's turret. Immediately, the Tiger's 88-mm (3.5-inch) cannon zeroed in on Bowen. As he scurried for the relative safety of a foxhole, a mortar round exploded next to him, badly wounding the American corporal. The tide of the fight turned against the American defenders and prisoners were taken, including Bowen. After receiving treatment for his wounds from a German doctor, Corporal Bowen was shipped off to a POW camp somewhere to the east. Similar scenarios of war played themselves out repeatedly during the siege of Bastogne.

To the north, the 7th armored division situated to guard St. Vith saw the size of the defense force increase on December 19. The 28th division's 112th regimental combat team made contact with a patrol of the 7th armored and set up positions as part of the protective line of American units protecting St. Vith. Most of the roads in the region were in American hands, crossing the middle of the advance line of the German offensive, from St. Vith south to Troisvierges. According to Toland's book, by the evening of Tuesday, December 19,

> the St. Vith salient was beginning to show signs of order though it consisted of only one armored division, a truncated and shaken infantry division, a separate regiment and armored combat command—and was provided minimum field artillery support. . . . But already Manteuffel's attack on St. Vith was three days behind schedule.[74]

The following day, however, the Germans were concentrating forces to capture St. Vith as quickly as possible, including elements of the 18th and 62nd volks-grenadier divisions, which had been assigned the capture of St. Vith in the first place, plus units of the 1st SS Panzer division. The 18th and 62nd concentrated on attacking Clarke's positions at St. Vith directly and other American defense positions located to the south. The 116th Panzer division attacked the U.S. 424th infantry at the town of Reuland, less than ten miles (16 kilometers) south of St. Vith.

By evening on December 20, the St. Vith salient was still firmly in American hands and making the German high command nervous. The tenacious American units entrenched in the German advance's center were keeping the 5th and 6th Panzer armies from linking together. The American-controlled roads in the region kept the offensive routes to the east jammed with German vehicles filled with gasoline and ammunition, unable to reach the Wehrmacht units that had advanced ahead to the west. In addition, because Generals Manteuffel and Model had to commit additional units to the St. Vith salient to try to break the American defense of the region, the two commanders were unable to dispatch those key fighting elements elsewhere in the ranging battle for the Ardennes. To provide additional German force against St. Vith, General "Sepp" Dietrich gave orders to his 2nd SS Panzer korps to turn to the south in support of Manteuffel's plans to throw his entire strength against the Americans. A massive attack was planned for December 21, the following day. All through the night of December 20–21, wrote Toland, "American troops in St. Vith could hear vehicles massing to the northeast and to the south. The time was coming near."[75]

It came late on the morning of December 21, at 11:00 A.M. Wehrmacht artillery fell across the eastern edge and northern portion of both General Clarke's and Hoge's positions. Two hours later, "the entire line was aflame with German artillery, rockets, tanks, and infantry."[76] The right flank of the 7th armored division's line began to appear vulnerable, but reserve units were dispatched to shore up the sagging defenses of Hoge's 9th armored.

As the day dragged on, though, the German assaults became relentless. By late in the afternoon, the Wehrmacht forces launched three massive assaults, each concentrating on a different road leading into St. Vith. Each one was preceded by heavy artillery shelling, sometimes lasting as long as half an hour and at 5:00 P.M., German tanks and infantry advanced down the Schonberg Road in a straight line out of the east. An hour and a half later, German units approached from the Malmedy Road to the north. By 8:00 P.M., the Prum Road to the southeast witnessed yet another enemy attack.

Throughout the afternoon, despite the heavy German advances, the American defense line held with only a few enemy troops breaking past. By 7:00 P.M., however, the German attack showed no signs of letting up, and for the next hour, a barrage of tank, bazooka, and machine-gun fire continued to light up the night sky across the Ardennes forest. American bazooka and machine-gun teams were blasted to bits, only to be replaced by another team. As Toland wrote, "as soon as one team was wiped out it was replaced by another, which was killed in turn a few minutes later."[77] By 10:00 P.M., after 11 hours of fighting, the Americans began to pull back, having taken all the German firepower they could. Casualties ran high, and already eight German tanks had reached the town of St. Vith, followed closely by units of Wehrmacht infantry. Lieutenant Colonel Tom Riggs contacted General Clarke by radio, giving him a report on the situation. Less than an hour later, Clarke responded: "Reform; save what vehicles you can; attack to the west to St. Vith; we are forming a new line west of town."[78] But the battle was lost. Lieutenant Colonel Riggs and hundreds of other U.S. troops were soon captured as prisoners of war and St. Vith was in enemy hands. Many of those who escaped German capture only did so because, as the Germans entered St. Vith, a traffic jam of Wehrmacht vehicles clogged the main streets and roads, reducing the enemy advance to a crawl. The town itself had been reduced to rubble by the heavy fighting; there were few buildings left standing.

American prisoners of war captured in the Ardennes. Sort of a "bulge within a bulge," the late-December salient at the town of St. Vith saw heavy fire on both sides before the Germans proved victorious. This battle led to the formation of the "Fortified Goose Egg" defense.

To the west of St. Vith was the road through Rodt to Poteau to Vielsalm. With the routing of American forces out of St. Vith, the Americans began organizing a new defense perimeter, a large oval-shaped piece of land measuring nearly ten miles (16 kilometers) across that would soon be referred to as the "Fortified Goose Egg."

Inside this defense field were the remaining elements of the 7th armored and the 106th divisions which, according to author Toland, "would remain in place, surrounded and cut off from other friendly forces and supplied by air."[79] The plan for the "goose egg" defense issued from Major General Matthew B. Ridgway, the commander of 18th airborne corps. Generals Hasbrouck and Clarke were not excited about the plan, their forces were worn out from a long day of fighting and they needed rest. Clarke even referred to the plan as "Custer's Last Stand."

Despite their opposition to the plan, the two field generals could not expect General Ridgway to change his mind. The general was a tough soldier (West Point class of 1917), and he did not compromise in the field. His image was a serious-minded veteran of combat, whose trademark was a "harness with grenades fastened to the front."[80] Ridgway was not a desk general, but sometimes enjoyed participating in patrols in search of tanks. More than once, Ridgway had fired his personal bazooka and knocked out a German Panzer. His paratroopers respected him greatly, and they saw him as a soldier's soldier. He was so matter-of-fact as a commander that he once observed: "A general is no less expendable than anyone else. In fact it might be good for morale if the troops saw a dead general now and then."[81] Now Ridgway was ordering a desperate stand to the west of St. Vith.

By December 21, Peiper's situation was extremely desperate. He was locked into the Stoumont region with no way out. The Panzer general called a meeting around noon with his battalion commanders just east of Stoumont, and the decision was made to abandon the town and retreat back to La Gleize. This move provided little respite for Peiper's beleaguered forces, since American artillery fire remained trained on the 50-house hamlet.

At every turn — Trois Ponts, Cheneux — Peiper could find no way out of his situation.

On the night of December 22, Luftwaffe planes tried to drop 1.5 tons of fuel to Peiper, which he needed desperately, but the attempt brought disastrous results. The drums of oil and gasoline were dropped over Stoumont, but Peiper had left that town and moved two miles (three kilometers) east. The German petroleum fell at a site occupied by the U.S. 30th division, instead. Following this, an all-out effort was launched to dispatch German forces to rescue Peiper from his entrapment. All were repulsed, except for one Panzer grenadier unit. By December 23, Peiper's men faced relentless attacks from the U.S. 30th and 3rd armored divisions. As one report later stated: "For breakfast . . . we got a double helping of artillery and mortar fire."[82] Finally, at noon, Peiper received a radio message giving him permission to retreat back to the east, but he still had no gasoline.

Nevertheless, with no options left short of surrender, Peiper and his battle group, now reduced to just 800 combatants, tried to make a break out of their predicament under cover of darkness on the morning of December 24, Christmas Eve, leaving behind "countless dead, 400 wounded and almost all of the division's panzer regiment."[83] Ironically, while Peiper's men had advanced under cover of the most powerful tanks of the German military under the command of the brashest of the Wehrmacht's Panzer commanders, those who remained alive from Peiper's battle group escaped back to the east on foot. As for General Dietrich's SS Panzer army to the north, they were stuck, having fought until they could proceed no farther.

By December 22, the Germans offered the Americans defending Bastogne an opportunity to surrender. They had surrounded the 101st airborne division for two days. The offer came from the Wehrmacht commander of

German forces intent on capturing Bastogne, General Heinrich Freiherr von Luttwitz. Luttwitz hoped to avoid a full-pitched battle by having the Americans surrender their garrison positions, as other American units had done earlier in the offensive. Inside Bastogne, General Anthony McAuliffe was assessing his situation that day. He later recalled the day: "Along about December twenty-second I was having my greatest doubts. Many were wounded and supplies were short. Some guns were down to ten rounds each."[84]

The offer was delivered by four Germans, including a major and a lieutenant, sent at 11:30 A.M. toward American units situated on the Arlon Road. A steady snow was falling. Spotting the approaching Germans, two American sergeants went out to meet them, along with a corpsman who spoke German. The Germans explained that they had an offer to deliver to the Americans' commanding officer. The Wehrmacht men were blindfolded and taken by jeep to a field headquarters. Their message was delivered through the American ranks until it reached the desk of Brigadier General Anthony McAuliffe at his headquarters in a cellar underneath the Heintz military barracks in Bastogne. The general was out in the field. He had to be tracked down and informed of the message from the Germans.

"What did they want?" asked McAuliffe.

The general's acting chief of staff, Colonel Ned D. Moore, answered: "They want us to surrender."

"Aw, nuts," said McAuliffe, as he read the German communiqué, which stated:

> To the U.S.A. Commander in the Encircled Town of Bastogne:
>   The fortune of war is changing. This time the U.S.A. forces in and near Bastogne have been encircled by strong German armored units. . . . There is only one

General Anthony McAuliffe commanded the 101st airborne division and was surrounded with his troops in the town of Bastogne. He turned down the opportunity to surrender with the irreverent yet succinct answer— "Nuts."

possibility to save the encircled U.S.A. troops from total annihilation: that is the honorable surrender of the encircled town. In order to think it over, a term of two hours will be granted beginning with the presentation of this note. . . . If this proposal should be rejected one German artillery corps and six heavy A.A. battalions are ready to annihilate the U.S.A. troops in and near Bastogne. . . . All the serious civilian losses caused by this artillery fire would not correspond with the well-known American humanity.[85]

McAuliffe was not interested in surrendering. As he considered an appropriate response to the German surrender proposal, one of his staff spoke up: "That first remark of yours would be hard to beat."

"What was that?" McAuliffe wondered.

"You said 'nuts,'" said Lieutenant Colonel Harry W. O. Kinnard.

"That's it!" said McAuliffe, enthusiastically. As he took a pen in hand, he scribbled the handwritten reply:

> 22 December 1944
> To the German Commander:
> N U T S !
> The American Commander

McAuliffe handed his written response to Colonel Joseph H. Harper, commander of the 327th. "See that this is forwarded to the Germans."

"I'll hand it over myself," said Harper. "It will be a lot of fun."[86]

Harper delivered the oddly worded response to the still blindfolded Germans and sent them back to their lines. The Americans would not be leaving Bastogne without a fight. The day of fighting on December 22 had

How do you say "NUTS!" in German?

On December 22 when General McAuliffe responded to the German request to surrender, his one word response—*NUTS!*—was not immediately understood by Germans, who were unfamiliar with American slang.

When his reply was read by German field emissaries, they did not understand its meaning even though they could read English. As they understood the word, *nuts* were "things you cracked. All this made little sense under the circumstances." *

The Germans requested an explanation: "Is the reply affirmative or negative?" they asked. Perhaps the Americans had not understood the German request. One of the German officers who had delivered the surrender request insisted that the two sides negotiate further but the Americans were finished. Colonel Joseph Harper, the U.S. officer who took McAuliffe's brief but straightforward response to the waiting Germans, assured them of the nature of his commander's response: "It is decidedly not affirmative." **

Blindfolding them once again, Harper escorted the Germans back to the site where they had emerged from the Ardennes fog to deliver their ultimatum. As he spoke to them for the final time, he drove home the point of McAuliffe's response.

"If you don't understand what NUTS means," he stated clearly, "in plain English it is the same as 'Go to Hell.' And I will tell you something else: if you continue to attack, we will kill every . . . damned German who tries to break into this city." ***

As the Germans saluted and prepared to return to their units, one spoke up in anger: "We will kill many Americans. This is war."

Colonel Harper, tired of dealing with them, dismissed the Germans, saying to them: "On your way, Bud." Then, as they started to leave, Harper said one more thing, a mysterious statement: "And good luck to you." ****

Years later, the American officer could not imagine what he had been thinking.

---

* *Source:* Quoted in Danny S. Parker, *Battle of the Bulge: Hitler's Ardennes Offensive, 1944–1945.* Conshohocken, PA: Combined Publishing, 1991, p. 175.

** *Source:* Ibid., p. 176.

*** *Source:* Ibid.

**** *Source:* Ibid.

marked a turning point in the fight for the Ardennes, and the American refusal to surrender Bastogne proved to be the climax of the Battle of the Bulge. There were many fights remaining in the last major German offensive of World War II, though. The soldier in the field understood this singular fact, and the commanders at supreme Allied headquarters knew it, too. On December 22, General Eisenhower issued an "Order of the Day," an uncommon action on his part. In the declaration, he encouraged all Allied forces in the Ardennes to "rise to new heights of courage, of resolution and of effort. . . . By rushing out from his fixed defense the enemy may give us the chance to turn his great gamble into his worst defeat."[87]

Before the end of the day, General von Manteuffel launched an attack to the west in hopes that his 5th Panzer army might reach the banks of the Meuse River. With St. Vith in German hands, the 66th armeekorps began assaulting Allied positions to the west in the region of Vielsalm and the Salm River, and Rodt fell to the Germans. The men of the U.S. 7th armored fought as strongly as they had when they occupied St. Vith the day before, but the situation for the 7th, locked in the "Fortified Goose Egg," was becoming desperate. General Ridgway received orders from his superior to abandon the field between St. Vith and Vielsalm. He was not happy with the order; neither was the commander of the 82nd airborne, Major General James W. Gavin, whose forces were inside the goose egg, as well. Gavin declared: "The division had never withdrawn throughout all its battles."[88] Once Ridgway inspected the American positions inside the oval-shaped defensive position with its limited roads and its defenders' lack of mobility, however, even the battle-hardened commander knew it was time to evacuate the defensive pocket.

How would he get 20,000 men out of their vulnerable field position with enemy elements surrounding them at nearly every turn, though? The withdrawal was set for Saturday morning, December 23. Examinations of the main road out of the goose egg revealed what everyone already knew, wrote Eisenhower: "the mud had made the roads impassable for armored vehicles."[89] Fortunately for the desperate Americans, however, freezing temperatures in the early morning hours froze the roads, allowing for the movement of even heavy vehicles. By 7:00 A.M., the armored units were moving, with General Clarke "standing at the crossroads in the village of Kommanster, once more directing traffic."[90] By 10:00 A.M., the majority of the American forces inside the "egg" had passed beyond Kommanster. That afternoon, the 7th armored division was at Xhoris, within the relative safety of American lines.

Only then could the losses of the 7th armored division, plus those of the 14th cavalry group that had been attached to the 7th, be assessed. Casualties ran to 3,400 men and officers killed, wounded, or missing. Eighty-eight tanks had been destroyed, as well as 25 armored cars. German losses were lighter, but the American stand at St. Vith had cost the Wehrmacht forces six precious days of fighting that had kept them from reaching the Meuse. Perhaps the Germans had been too cautious in engaging the 7th armored. The numbers of German combatants had been far greater, and on December 17, at the opening of the German assaults at St. Vith, General Clarke had only had 2,500 men available to hold his position in the path of the enemy. Twenty years after the war, General Clarke met with the Wehrmacht General von Manteuffel and asked him why he had not pressed a direct frontal assault against the Americans earlier. Manteuffel's answer was direct, analytical, and extremely revealing. His answer to Clarke's question might explain why the overall Watch on the Rhine counteroffensive, Adolf Hitler's cockeyed dream to swing the war back in his favor, ultimately failed to reach its long-range objectives:

> We estimated that we were up against a division, and perhaps against an entire corps. We made several probing attacks, and every time we went into your position, we encountered armor. Our preliminary briefings had told us that there would be no armor in our path. When you get surprised like this, you become cautious.[91]

In the end, the Battle of the Bulge may have been won by the extraordinary field mobility of America's fighting men and equipment, as well as its commanders.

The skies above Bastogne cleared on December 23 and Allied planes were able to fly over the besieged city, after having been grounded during the previous week. Bombers struck enemy-held bridges and rail yards, as well as armored columns sitting in vulnerable positions on open roads. As one German observer said, "Airplanes everywhere. Thousands. . . . I didn't see a single Luftwaffe plane."[92] Not only did the Allied aircraft drop bombs and ordnance on the Germans, but they also parachuted supplies to the Americans trapped in Bastogne, including medicine, food, blankets, ammunition, and especially artillery shells. The drops were right on their targets. Ninety percent of the supplies shoved out of cargo planes and parachuted to the ground reached the desperate American troops.

The German assaults against the American defenses surrounding Bastogne continued, each growing a little stronger. The Wehrmacht's Christmas Eve attack was especially heavy. These thrusts brought no overwhelming victory and even little field advancement against the men of the 101st airborne and the 10th armored, whose morale and fighting capacity had just been resupplied from the sky the day before.

On Christmas Day, both armies celebrated as best they could, although no cease-fire was called. Turkey dinners were sent out to as many Americans involved in the defense of Bastogne as possible. For a lot of the men at the frontlines, it was a meal of white beans, and for some at the front, their food arrived frozen. General McAuliffe had located a printing press somewhere in the town and had a Christmas card printed and handed out to his men. His message was as hopeful as the season called for and as realistic:

> What's merry about all this, you ask? Just this: We have stopped cold everything that has been thrown at us. . . . We are giving our country and our loved ones at home a worthy Christmas present and being privileged to take part in this gallant feat of arms and truly making for ourselves a merry Christmas.[93]

The Wehrmacht did launch one of its most intense attacks that day, but it was a miserable failure.

The next day brought a great turn of events in Bastogne. For days, Patton's 3rd army had been slogging its way toward the besieged Ardennes town from the south. Patton had promised that his men would reach Bastogne by Christmas but they had not. Then, on December 26, a bright clear day with open skies, his spearhead unit, the 4th armored division's 37th tank battalion, with air cover provided by P-47s, broke through German lines and reached the village. The first tanks of Patton's army rolled into Bastogne around 4:50 P.M. Thirty-three-year-old Lieutenant Charles Boggess commanded the first

An antiaircraft gun and team watched Allied and Axis planes in the skies over Puffendorf, near Aachen, Germany. The Allied air forces helped win World War II against a German Luftwaffe that had been severely and permanently depleted by the Battle of the Bulge.

armored vehicle to link up with the 101st airborne, which had taken everything the Germans had to throw against Bastogne and had held out. His Sherman tank was escorted by eight others and he had already met up with units of the 101st airborne outside the town. Excitement spread quickly among the men of the 101st and the 10th armored all along the perimeter line around the town. General McAuliffe came out to the perimeter to greet the advance units of Patton's 3rd army. One of the 37th tank commanders, Captain William Dwight, spoke to McAuliffe: "How are you, General?"

"Gee, I am mighty glad to see you," said McAuliffe.[94]

With Patton's 3rd army already in Bastogne by December 23, German commander Manteuffel, who had pushed the 7th armored out of St. Vith, could no longer proceed toward the Meuse River. With Patton to contend with, all

Manteuffel could do was divert his struggling units to turn on the defensive and resist an increasing wave of American forces. Only one small German force was able to reach the vicinity of the Meuse, coming to within four miles (six kilometers) of the all-important river, near the town of Dinant, but these forces were quickly annihilated by the Allies. Though Manteuffel called up German artillery to provide him cover, it never arrived. There was no fuel to bring the powerful German guns to the frontline.

The skies above the Ardennes were clear on December 23, which only complicated the German offensive by further allowing the Allies to heavily bomb German field positions, while the Luftwaffe remained largely grounded. Many Luftwaffe aircraft had been lost, and those needing to take to the skies could not find fuel.

Even as Patton pushed his operations along the southern flank of the German lines, General Bernard Montgomery was directing the Allied effort to the north. By December 26, the Germans could push forward no more. Those German units that had formed the spearhead—the legendary "bulge" in the Allied lines—began to fall back, their gasoline tanks empty.

The excellent leadership of the Allied commanders was a leading factor in the defeat of Hitler's German army in the Battle of the Bulge. Seen here in this 1944 photograph, in the front row from left to right are General George Patton, General Omar Bradley, and General Dwight Eisenhower, surrounded by a group of their colleagues.

Epilogue

By December 26, the battle for the Ardennes had been decided; German units were retreating up and down their ragged advance line. With the turnaround in the Ardennes, Allied commanders systematically shifted their resources and manpower to squeeze the remaining German troops out during the final days of December and early January 1945. The reality of the battlefield—that the German Wehrmacht had lost its gamble to break through the American-held forest region, cross the Meuse with impunity, and then roll into the city of Antwerp—had finally reached across the distances to the east and German high command. Those German leaders had decisions of their own to make: They encouraged Hitler to accept the defeat of his Watch on the Rhine and regroup his forces, spearhead a new assault to the north, swing to the west of Liege, and strike Aachen. This plan was basically the same one Wehrmacht commanders had encouraged the führer to pursue two months earlier—the attack plan that had been labeled the "Small Solution." Hitler's focus was still riveted on the Ardennes, though. He still expected the town of Bastogne to be taken, and Antwerp was still his goal. As the field situation in the Ardennes deteriorated further, however, even the out-of-touch Nazi leader finally had to admit defeat. As the year 1945 opened, author Griess wrote:

> Hitler even acknowledged that his offensive could not succeed. The final attack on Bastogne took place on January 3 and 4. . . . When it was repulsed, Model ordered an SS panzer division north to defend against the attack of the 1st army, which had begun as sched-uled on January 3. On the eighth, Hitler authorized a withdrawal to the Ourthe River.[95]

January brought the Ardennes counteroffensive to an end. Montgomery had ordered forces under his command to move forward in the north on January 3. Winter weather over the next two weeks slowed the Allied advance to the east, but by January 16, northern and southern field units met up at Houffalize. The following day, General Bradley regained command of the 1st army, and by January 28, the bulge created by German advances first launched 44 days earlier had been eliminated. Meanwhile, Hitler had to focus on a new crisis in the field. Soviet forces to the east mounted a major offensive toward Germany on January 12, and he soon dispatched the remnants of the 6th SS Panzer army, battered and fresh from defeat in the Ardennes, to meet the Soviet threat.

The Battle of the Bulge had been an epic struggle in the annals of military history. Great armies of scope had engaged in weeks of mechanized combat under brutal winter conditions on a field of battle that constantly threw up obstacles blocking their mobility and ability to even reach the enemy. Three German armies had engaged in the Watch on the Rhine offensive, a combined force of 500,000 men, but one out of every five became a casualty. The American army suffered a staggering 81,000 casualties during the Battle of the Bulge, including 19,000 killed and 15,000 captured. (The British, who only entered the fighting in the final stages of the hard-fought offensive, tallied 1,400 casualties.)

Many of the towns nestled in the Ardennes were utterly destroyed by this final major battle in the Western theater of the war, including St. Vith. Scattered up and down the roads, farm lanes, and wooded regions of the Ardennes were the destroyed hulks of German and American vehicles, including tanks, jeeps, armored cars, trucks, and artillery pieces. The Panzer divisions that Hitler had unleashed into the dark forests of the Ardennes that winter would never be replaced. For the German air force, the story was the same: The Luftwaffe had lost hundreds of invaluable aircraft that could only be written off. Both sides had destroyed approximately 800 tanks of their enemy's, but the Americans were able to replace all their losses in no time at all.

For the commanders who led the Wehrmacht forces into the wintry hell of the Ardennes, they could take little comfort in emerging from the offensive knowing they had been right, that the counteroffensive laid out by

Adolf Hitler had been untenable, unmanageable, and doomed. As the offensive drew to a close, those who had survived the fruitless campaign understood that the war was lost, that the Allies would push into their homeland from the west just as the Soviets were preparing to strike toward the heart of Germany from the east. The next five months, from December until May, would represent the bitter end of a war that would witness the destruction of Germany and its people, as well as its leader. Adolf Hitler would commit suicide at the end of April, just 48 hours before the complete surrender of all German military forces.

For the American military leaders, from Eisenhower down to the squad leaders and tank commanders who met the German offensive during those bloody days in mid-December, the Battle of the Bulge was both a major victory and a setback. After having made extraordinary progress during the previous six months following the June 6 D day invasion, the offensive in the Ardennes probably threw off the Allied plans to invade Germany directly by as many as six weeks. The Americans nevertheless emerged from the offensive with a stronger reputation for war than many, including Hitler, had ever recognized, according to writer Hastings:

> The Ardennes campaign was, from beginning to end, an American battle and an American triumph. During the struggle from the beaches of Normandy, there had been moments for doubting the quality of the American soldier. Hitler described the Americans contemptuously as "the Allies' Italians." In the battle for the Ardennes, however, against the finest troops Germany could still put into the field, the US army showed a new skill and maturity as a fighting force.[96]

No one summed up the importance of the Battle of the Bulge to the American army better than British Prime Minister Winston Churchill, who stated succinctly: "the Ardennes was the greatest American battle of the war."[97]

1933   Adolf Hitler rises to power in Germany.

1936   Germany and Italy form an alliance called the Rome-Berlin Axis.

1938   German forces the annexation of Austria, a direct violation of the Versailles Treaty; Germany annexes the Sudetenland of Czechoslovakia.

1939   Hitler orders his forces to invade Poland; England and France declare war on Germany; World War II begins.

1940   German troops carry out successful "blitzkrieg" advances against Belgium, Holland, and Luxembourg; France falls to the Nazis; England fights the Battle of Britain against Hitler's "Operation Sea Lion."

1941   Hitler orders the invasion of the Soviet Union; Japan attacks Pearl Harbor; the United States declares war on Japan, Germany, and Italy.

1942–1943   German forces are driven out of northern Africa by combined forces of British and Americans.

1944

June 6   Allied forces land at Normandy to drive the Germans from Western Europe.

July 20   Wehrmacht officers make an assassination attempt on Adolf Hitler, who survives.

July 31   Americans break out of their Normandy beachheads after seven weeks of fighting.

September 16   Hitler meets with high-ranking commanders and announces his plans for a winter offensive in Western Europe.

October 11   German Colonel General Alfred Jodl, chief of operations, presents "Christrose," his version of an Ardennes Offensive, to Hitler.

October 27   German military leaders Rundstedt and Model present revamped offensive—the "Small Solution"—to Hitler as scaled-down version of the Ardennes Offensive; Hitler rejects their proposals.

October 21   Hitler meets with his high command concerning details of the Ardennes Offensive, now called Watch on the Rhine; he discusses plans for "Operation Grief" with his favorite commando, Otto Skorzeny.

September 4   British tank General Bernard Montgomery and his forces reach the city of Antwerp, the ultimate target of Hitler's planned offensive.

September 17   Montgomery launches his "Operation Market-Garden" into Holland.

December 11   Hitler meets with his top commanders just days before the launching of Watch on the Rhine.

December 16   Germans launch the Watch on the Rhine offensive into the Ardennes forest at 5:30 A.M.; by the end of first day of the German blitz into the Ardennes, Hitler's timetable for advance is already behind schedule.

December 17   The first units of the U.S. 17th armored division reach Bastogne; the bulk of the 7th armored is already on its way toward St. Vith; that evening, German Generals Model and Manteuffel are disappointed in the lack of progress into the Ardennes, but the day ends with several American positions routed and thousands of U.S. soldiers on the run; Malmedy Massacre takes place; one of Skorzeny's jeep teams reaches the Meuse River.

December 18   The number of retreating U.S. forces increases from the previous day; General Peiper's tanks reach the town of Stavelot, only to have his advance stymied by a lack of fuel; 2nd Panzer division stands six miles north of Bastogne; another day ends with the German high command displeased with the offensive's lack of progress.

December 19   German field armies are facing a serious fuel shortage; promised fuel supplies are never delivered; Eisenhower meets with his senior commanders and orders Patton's 3rd army to move north toward Bastogne by December 22 or 23; Wehrmacht General Dietrich continues to face stiff American opposition, nearly halting his 6th Panzer army; German Panzers prepare to surround Bastogne just as the men of the U.S. 101st airborne division reach the town.

December 20   St. Vith is still in American hands, upsetting the German high command; a massive German attack is planned for the following day against American forces at St. Vith.

December 21   A massive German assault against St. Vith is launched, forcing the American to evacuate the town and take up positions to the west; Peiper's situation becomes extremely desperate, as he is locked in the Stoumont region with no way out, and fuel is running low.

December 22   Luftwaffe attempts to drop 4,500 tons of fuel to Peiper, which fails to reach him and falls into the hands of the U.S. 30th armored division instead; at Bastogne, the Germans demand the surrender of General McAuliffe and his 101st airborne division; his reply: "Nuts!"

December 23   The U.S. 30th armored and the 3rd armored division relentlessly attack Peiper's columns; Peiper is ordered to retreat back to the east, but does not have enough fuel to complete his evacuation from the field; evacuation of U.S. defenders at St. Vith is ordered.

December 26   Elements of Patton's 3rd army reach Bastogne; German units that had formed the "bulge" spearhead in the Ardennes begin pulling out of the region; the battle for the Ardennes has been decided in the Americans' favor.

December 28   After 44 days of fighting, the German "bulge" in the Ardennes has been completely eliminated.

1945

January 8   Hitler authorizes a withdrawal of all German troops out of the Ardennes.

CHAPTER ONE: AN EXPANDING GLOBAL CONFLICT

1. Quoted in John Toland, *Adolf Hitler*. Garden City, NY: Doubleday & Company, Inc., 1976, p. 158.
2. Quoted in Stephen Ambrose, *American Heritage New History of World War II*. New York: Viking, 1997, p. 23.

CHAPTER TWO: FROM NORMANDY TO THE ARDENNES

3. Quoted in Stephen Ambrose, *Citizen Soldiers: The U.S. Army from the Normandy Beaches to the Bulge to the Surrender of Germany, June 7, 1944–May 7, 1945*. New York: Simon & Schuster, 1997, p. 69.
4. Quoted in John Toland, *Battle: The Story of the Bulge*. New York: Random House, 1969, p. 14.
5. Ibid.
6. Quoted in Lieutenant Colonel Eddy Bauer, *Illustrated World War II Encyclopedia*. New York: H. S. Stuttman Inc., 1978, p. 1964.
7. Quoted in Danny S. Parker, *Battle of the Bulge: Hitler's Ardennes Offensive, 1944–1945*. Conshohocken, PA: Combined Publishing, 1991, p. 22.
8. Ibid.
9. Ibid.
10. Quoted in John Toland, *Adolf Hitler*. Garden City, NY: Doubleday & Company, Inc., 1976, p. 830.
11. Quoted in Bruce Quarrie, *The Ardennes Offensive*. Oxford, UK: Osprey Publishing, 1999, p. 10.
12. Quoted in Toland, *Bulge*, p. 15.
13. Quoted in Toland, *Hitler*, p. 830.
14. Quoted in Toland, *Bulge*, p. 16.

CHAPTER THREE: "WATCH ON THE RHINE"

15. Quoted in John Toland, *Battle: The Story of the Bulge*. New York: Random House, 1969, p. 17.
16. Quoted in Colonel Ernest Dupuy, *World War II, A Compact History*. New York: Hawthorn Books, Inc., 1969, p. 198.
17. Quoted in Danny S. Parker, *Battle of the Bulge: Hitler's Ardennes Offensive, 1944–1945*. Conshohocken, PA: Combined Publishing, 1991, p. 49.
18. Ibid.
19. Ibid.
20. Quoted in Max Hastings, *Victory in Europe*. Boston: Little, Brown and Company, 1985, p. 101.
21. Quoted in John S. D. Eisenhower, *The Bitter Woods*. New York: G. P. Putnam's Sons, 1969, p. 150.

22. Ibid., pp. 150–151.
23. Quoted in Toland, *Bulge*, p. 21.

CHAPTER FOUR: INTO THE WOODS

24. Quoted in John Toland, *Battle: The Story of the Bulge*. New York: Random House, 1969, p. 23.
25. Ibid., p. 26.
26. Quoted in Stephen Ambrose, *Citizen Soldiers: The U.S. Army from the Normandy Beaches to the Bulge to the Surrender of Germany, June 7, 1944–May 7, 1945*. New York: Simon & Schuster, 1997, p. 187.
27. Quoted in Thomas E. Griess, *The Second World War: Europe and the Mediterranean*. Wayne, NJ: Avery Publishing Group, Inc., 1984, p. 378.
28. Quoted in Danny S. Parker, *Battle of the Bulge: Hitler's Ardennes Offensive, 1944–1945*. Conshohocken, PA: Combined Publishing, 1991, p. 67.
29. Ibid., p. 68.
30. Ibid.
31. Quoted in Ambrose, p. 188.
32. Ibid., p. 200.
33. Quoted in Toland, *Bulge*, p. 41.
34. Quoted in Parker, p. 378.
35. Quoted in Ambrose, p. 200.
36. Ibid.
37. Ibid., p. 197.
38. Ibid., p. 190.
39. Quoted in Parker, p. 83.
40. Ibid., p. 82.
41. Ibid., p. 83.
42. Quoted in Ambrose, p. 199.
43. Quoted in Toland, *Bulge*, p. 48.
44. Quoted in John S. D. Eisenhower, *The Bitter Woods*. New York: G. P. Putnam's Sons, 1969, p. 233.
45. Ibid.
46. Ibid., p. 234.
47. Ibid., p. 235.
48. Ibid.
49. Ibid., p. 239.
50. Quoted in Ambrose, p. 202.
51. Quoted in Parker, p. 107.
52. Quoted in Ambrose, pp. 204–205.

CHAPTER FIVE: "WHAT'S A TEXAS LEAGUER?"

53. Quoted in Danny S. Parker, *Battle of the Bulge: Hitler's Ardennes Offensive, 1944–1945*. Conshohocken, PA: Combined Publishing, 1991, p. 109, Footnote #6.
54. Ibid. p. 109.
55. Ibid., p. 113.
56. Ibid.

57. Ibid.
58. Ibid.
59. Quoted in Stephen Ambrose, *Citizen Soldiers: The U.S. Army from the Normandy Beaches to the Bulge to the Surrender of Germany, June 7, 1944–May 7, 1945.* New York: Simon & Schuster, 1997, p. 208.
60. Quoted in John S. D. Eisenhower, *The Bitter Woods.* New York: G. P. Putnam's Sons, 1969, pp. 256–257.
61. Quoted in Lieutenant Colonel Eddy Bauer, *Illustrated World War II Encyclopedia.* New York: H. S. Stuttman Inc., 1978, p. 1979.
62. Quoted in Eisenhower, p. 257.
63. Ibid.
64. Quoted in Parker, p. 134.
65. Ibid., p. 135.
66. Ibid., p. 170.
67. Ibid.
68. Ibid.
69. Ibid.
70. Ibid., p. 171.
71. Ibid., p. 172.

CHAPTER SIX: "NUTS!"

72. Quoted in Stephen Ambrose, *Citizen Soldiers: The U.S. Army from the Normandy Beaches to the Bulge to the Surrender of Germany, June 7, 1944–May 7, 1945.* New York: Simon & Schuster, 1997, p. 223.
73. Ibid.
74. Quoted in John Toland, *Battle: The Story of the Bulge.* New York: Random House, 1969, p. 287.
75. Ibid., p. 294.

76. Ibid.
77. Ibid., p. 297.
78. Ibid.
79. Ibid., p. 299.
80. Ibid.
81. Ibid., p. 301.
82. Quoted in Danny S. Parker, *Battle of the Bulge: Hitler's Ardennes Offensive, 1944–1945.* Conshohocken, PA: Combined Publishing, 1991, p. 178.
83. Ibid., p. 184.
84. Ibid., p. 166.
85. Ibid., p. 175.
86. Ibid., pp. 173–174.
87. Ibid., p. 163.
88. Ibid., p. 164.
89. Quoted in John S. D. Eisenhower, *The Bitter Woods.* New York: G. P. Putnam's Sons, 1969, p. 302.
90. Ibid.
91. Ibid., p. 304.
92. Quoted in Ambrose, p. 225.
93. Ibid., p. 237.
94. Ibid., p. 248.

EPILOGUE

95. Quoted in Thomas E. Griess, *The Second World War: Europe and the Mediterranean.* Wayne, NJ: Avery Publishing Group, Inc., 1984, p. 385.
96. Quoted in Max Hastings, *Victory in Europe.* Boston: Little, Brown and Company, 1985, p. 113.
97. Ibid., p. 114.

Ambrose, Stephen E. *American Heritage New History of World War II*. New York: Viking, 1997.

———. *Citizen Soldiers: The U.S. Army From the Normandy Beaches to the Bulge to the Surrender of Germany, June 7, 1944–May 7, 1945*. New York: Simon & Schuster, 1997.

———. *The Victors: Eisenhower and His Boys: The Men of World War II*. New York: Simon & Schuster, 1998.

Ayer, Fred, Jr. *Before the Colors Fade: Portrait of a Soldier, George S. Patton, Jr.* Boston: Houghton Mifflin Company, 1964.

Bauer, Lieutenant Colonel Eddy. *Illustrated World War II Encyclopedia, Volume 15*. New York: H. S. Stuttman, Inc., Publishers, 1978.

Bradley, Omar N. *A Soldier's Story*. New York: Henry Holt and Company, 1951.

Bullock, Alan. *Hitler and Stalin: Parallel Lives*. New York: Alfred A. Knopf, 1992.

Dupuy, Colonel R. Ernest. *World War II: A Compact History*. New York: Hawthorn Books, Inc., 1969.

Eisenhower, Dwight D. *Crusade in Europe*. New York: Doubleday & Company, 1948.

Eisenhower, John S. D. *The Bitter Woods*. New York: G. P. Putnam's Sons, 1969.

Griess, Thomas E. *The Second World War: Europe and the Mediterranean*. Wayne, New Jersey: Avery Publishing Group, Inc., 1984.

Hastings, Max. *Victory in Europe: D-Day to VE Day in Full Color*. Boston: Little, Brown & Company, 1985.

Hirshson, Stanley P. *General Patton: A Soldier's Life*. New York: HarperCollins Publishers, 2002.

Merriam, Robert E. *The Battle of the Bulge: Hitler's Last Desperate Gamble to Win the War!* New York: Ballantine Books, 1978.

Noakes, Jeremy, and Geoffrey Pridham, eds., *Nazism, 1919–1945*. New York: Exeter, 1983.

Parker, Danny S. *Battle of the Bulge: Hitler's Ardennes Offensive, 1944–45*. Conshohocken, PA: Combined Publishing, 1991.

Quarrie, Bruce. *The Ardennes Offensive*. Oxford, UK: Osprey Publishing, 1999.

Speer, Albert. *Inside the Third Reich*. New York: Macmillan Company, 1970.

Toland, John. *Adolf Hitler*. Garden City, NY: Doubleday & Company, Inc., 1976.

———. *Battle: The Story of the Bulge*. New York: Random House, 1959.

page:

14: © Associated Press, AP
19: © Associated Press, AP
23: © Associated Press, AP
24: © Associated Press, U.S. ARMY
29: © Bettmann/CORBIS
32: © Associated Press, AP
34: © CORBIS
41: © CORBIS
45: © CORBIS
48: © Associated Press, U.S. ARMY
53: © Hulton|Archive, by Getty Images
58: © CORBIS

63: © CORBIS
65: © CORBIS
68: © Associated Press, AP
73: © Associated Press, AP
76: © Hulton|Archive, by Getty Images
83: © Hulton|Archive, by Getty Images
86: © Bettmann/CORBIS
88: © Associated Press, U.S. ARMY
95: © CORBIS
99: © CORBIS
106: © Associated Press, U.S. ARMY
108: © Associated Press, AP

Cover: © CORBIS

Frontis: Courtesy of the Library of Congress, Geography and Map Division

Tim McNeese is an Associate Professor of History at York College in Nebraska. He is the author of more than fifty books and educational materials on everything from Egyptian pyramids to American Indians. His audiences range from elementary students to adults. Professor McNeese graduated from York College with his Associate of Arts degree, as well as Harding University where he received his Bachelor of Arts degree in history and political science. He received his Master of Arts degree in history from Southwest Missouri State University. Professor McNeese's writing career has earned him a citation in the "Something About the Author" reference work. He is married to Beverly McNeese who teaches English at York College.

Caspar W. Weinberger was the fifteenth secretary of defense, serving under President Ronald Reagan from 1981 to 1987. Born in California in 1917, he fought in the Pacific during World War II then went on to pursue a law career. He became an active member of the California Republican Party and was named the party's chairman in 1962. Over the next decade, Weinberger held several federal government offices, including chairman of the Federal Trade Commission and secretary of health, education, and welfare. Ronald Reagan appointed him to be secretary of defense in 1981. He became one of the most respected secretaries of defense in history and served longer than any previous secretary except for Robert McNamara (who served 1961–1968). Today, Weinberger is chairman of the influential *Forbes* magazine.